WORK ETHICS AND THE GENERATION GAP!

Which Ethical Track Are You On?

BY

ROBIN L. RASK

authorHOUSE®

AuthorHouse™
1663 Liberty Drive, Suite 200
Bloomington, IN 47403
www.authorhouse.com
Phone: 1-800-839-8640

First published by AuthorHouse 5/15/2008

ISBN: 978-1-4343-2664-5 (sc)
ISBN: 978-1-4343-6404-3 (hc)

Printed in the United States of America
Bloomington, Indiana

This book is printed on acid-free paper.

Table Of Contents

WORK ETHICS TODAY AND THE GENERATION GAP
CONTENTS / OVERVIEW: IX
ACKNOWLEDGMENTS. XV

OPINIONS AND OBSEREVATIONS
WORK ETHICS TODAY & THE GENERATION GAP! 1

CHAPTER TWO
CUSTOMER SERVICE 19

CHAPTER THREE
INTEGRITY, SELF-RESPECT, AND SELF-ESTEEM 41

CHAPTER FOUR
GOALS AND PERSEVERANCE. 45

CHAPTER FIVE
MOTIVATION & AFFIRMATIONS 49

CHAPTER SIX
TIME MANAGEMENT & BALANCE 53

CHAPTER SEVEN
COMMUNITY OPINIONS ON WORK ETHICS TODAY! . . 59

CHAPTER EIGHT
EMPLOYER FEEDBACK & WORKER RIGHTS. 79

Chapter Nine

GENERATION X & Y.................................93

Chapter Ten

LEADING A MULTI-GENERATIONAL WORKFORCE.... 103

Chapter Eleven

CONCLUSION 107

Chapter Twelve/Additional Materials

AMERICAN GENERATIONS 109
TREATING CUSTOMERS WELL.......................115
THE BIG FIVE....................................119
ANOTHER APPROACH: THE INFORMATIONAL
INTERVIEW.......................................123
ROBIN'S ONE-PAGE RECIPE FOR FINDING A JOB!.....129
TEN MOST WANTED LIST 131
IF YOU'RE OFFERED THE JOB.......................133
HOW TO KEEP YOUR JOB 134
THE ABCS OF LOVING YOUR JOB 136
POSITIVE AFFIRMATIONS..........................140
RULES FOR STUDENTS 143
AMERICA'S DRUG PROBLEM!........................146
YOU MAY BE A WORKAHOLIC:.......................148
YOU ARE SO BLESSED!!...........................150
ABOUT THE AUTHOR 153

WORK ETHICS TODAY AND THE GENERATION GAP
CONTENTS / OVERVIEW:

CHAPTER ONE / WORK ETHICS TODAY

What happened to today's work ethics? So many students and adults seem to be lacking work ethics and responsibility. How can we change this and how do we get our families back together? Today's students will be our teachers and leaders of the future. One customer said, "'Work ethics' is an oxymoron."

CHAPTER TWO / CUSTOMER SERVICE

"The customer is always right." These are words that were first spoken by hotelier César Ritz. He began his career as a waiter at the age of sixteen and was fired four times. However, perseverance kept him going. Customer service is not what it use to be and not the same everywhere. Good and poor customer service has a great deal to do with our new generation working in these jobs. This chapter provides several examples of customer service.

CHAPTER THREE / INTEGRITY, SELF-RESPECT, AND SELF- ESTEEM

Integrity is doing the right thing even when no one is looking. Having integrity builds character. Character is something we demonstrate regularly. Not everyone does what he or she says they will do. Self-esteem is how you feel about yourself and the value you place on yourself. Thomas Edison and Einstein were both told they were dumb and were poor students. When someone tells you, "You can't," then your internal response can tell him or her, "I can." Poor self-esteem is something you can repair.

Using affirmations will help you to become a more positive person.

CHAPTER FOUR / GOALS AND PERSEVERANCE

It has been said, "If you fail to plan, you plan to fail." Without a goal or purpose, you have no direction. We need to take baby steps to where we want to go. Conduct informational interviews, research, and speak to those who are doing what you may want to do. A goal is a commitment to affect change. A goal needs to be something you want and something you see yourself doing. It needs to be specific: how much and by when? Everyone has problems sometimes in their lives; the only ones who do not are in heaven or that other place. It is important to keep your attitude positive, irrespective of whether things are going smoothly or not. It is worth remembering that Thomas Edison failed 32,000 times before his light bulb became viable. Consider the story about the farmer and his donkey that fell in a well: The very dirt that tried to bury him ended up saving his life.

CHAPTER FIVE / MOTIVATION AND AFFIRMATIONS

We all do what we want to do and what we do not want to do. Unmotivated people are that way because they choose not to be motivated. Motivation is the key to getting going. But how to get motivated? That is the question. Having a positive attitude is very important to being self-motivated. You need to determine what motivates you, then go after it. If you keep thinking about something in your mind, eventually, your body will end up going there, whether it is positive or negative. Imagine those moments when you are craving something sweet to eat.

Affirmations are positive statements about yourself. They are short, specific, and goal-oriented. Affirmations start with, "I am ..." or "I will ..." For example, "I will be living in a beach house by 2014." Begin saying what you are, what you want, and where you want to be as if it already is!

CHAPTER SIX / TIME MANAGEMENT AND BALANCE

Time management has a great deal to do with work ethics. Time is such a precious commodity. Time management has less to do with managing our time than learning to manage yourself more effectively. To state the obvious, there are 7 days in a week, and 168 hours in a week. It is the twenty-four hours that are key for us. Time management is about learning to set priorities and say NO! When it comes to balance, we all need to learn what our limits are and what our priorities are.

CHAPTER SEVEN / COMMUNITY OPINIONS ON WORK ETHICS TODAY

This chapter is all about different community members—teachers, parents, and employers—expressing their concerns and observations on the past and present generations of our students and adults in today's generation and workplace.

CHAPTER EIGHT / EMPLOYER FEEDBACK AND WORKER RIGHTS

Several students and adults have lost their jobs for various different reasons and some before they even began. Just to name a few of the reasons: not showing up, lateness, stealing, poor customer service, lack of respect, poor attitude, not following procedures, quitting, not being able to pass a drug test, etc. One student went to work and claimed he was there all day, when he actually clocked in and went out another door. One applicant was placed in an office for training and quit after six hours. She claimed it was too hard. All she had to do was answer telephones and take messages.

A college placement specialist had a student who needed a job and told her she wanted a job where she could sit and do her homework. One employer says, "When applicants come in to apply at his store, he asks them if they can take a drug test today?" The majority say, "Today is not a good day." This is a good way for the employer to weed out applicants who are not appropriate for hire. Some employees may be taken advantage of by their employers and not be aware of it. Enclosed are some of their rights that protect their working conditions by California Department of Industrial Labor Standards.

CHAPTER NINE / GENERATIONS X AND Y

Could generations X, and Y be a possible answer to our generation gap? Our generation today does not understand how we survived without the Internet, digital cameras, DVDs, cell phones, etc. Our present and future generations may not be able to relate to all the events in history that have occurred, such as the Gulf War, Desert Storm, the *Challenger* explosion, the L.A. riots, the Columbine shootings, the AIDS epidemic, September 11 and the Twin Towers attack, the war on terror, major hurricanes, etc. The 1920s, all the way to our new millennium, were all different eras in our lives.

Based on research defining generations X and Y, demographics have usually relied on the formative experiences of national events to characterize the generation groups. As far as work ethics goes, maybe we need to understand what generation we were born into and learn to adapt, and accept the fact that we are all unique.

CHAPTER TEN / LEADING A MULTI-GENERATIONAL WORKFORCE

Dr. Joanne Sujansky, founder of KEY group, author, and certified professional speaker, sheds some light on Generation X, Y, and the baby boomers. What shaped them, choices, training opportunities in the workplace, etc.

CHAPTER ELEVEN / CONCLUSION

When most of us went to school, we did not have all the work-experience programs and resources to help us that today's students have now. It seems today that most people want a job but do not want to really work. Think of how different our world and society would be if there was a mandatory semester of military training in our schools. Students would at least receive the structure and discipline they so desperately need.

Chapter Twelve / Additional Information, Materials, and Resources:

American Generations (Wikipedia)

Beloit College Wisconsin (Feeling Old List)

Treating Customers Well

The Big Five

Qualities of a Leader

Informational Interviews

Sources of Employment

Military Training Programs

Robin's One Page Recipe for Finding a Job!

10+ Most Wanted List (What Employers Are Looking For)

If You're Offered the Job

Leaving Your Job

The ABC's of Loving Your Job, by Dr. John C. Maxwell

100 Ways to Motivate Yourself, by Steve Chandler

Positive Affirmations

14 Rules for Students, by Charles Sykes

You May Be a Workaholic, Chuckles, by Donald E. Wetmore

America's Drug Problem

You Are So Blessed

ACKNOWLEDGMENTS

I want to thank all the wonderful people who provided their input to this project. Some of you are family and friends. Some of you are colleagues, and some of you I have never even met. I want to thank Robi Holland for some of the typing inserts you did for me for my job, so I was able to use a few for this book. I also want to thank Leslie Poulsen, who helped me edit a portion of this book. You are always there when I need you! I greatly appreciate **all of you** taking the time to voice your opinions on the subject of today's work ethics, which we hope will change in the future in a more positive way! I feel very blessed to have so many of you in my circle of family and great friends.

There are several others whom I have asked for input. These people said they would love to provide their input, however, they did not. Some I had to ask several times and they kept saying that they would. I understand that everyone is busy and has his or her own priorities. People, who are now people like me, say they will do things and they do them. "I love it." This somewhat proves my point regarding work ethics. "Sorry for those of you I may have offended."

Unfortunately, not everyone is a "now" person. In my *Self-Management to Time Management* book, I provide some suggestions on that topic. I know we are all unique, however, I find being a now person allows me to get everything done that I need to. As soon as I know I need to do something, I do it. When I am on the telephone at work or at home and someone wants me to send information, I do it as my next priority and then it is finished. If I know I need to take something with me the next day, I put it by my purse or in the car ASAP; otherwise, I may forget. I even call myself at work and leave messages for myself. I have a to-do list and call list by my phone, and at home, I have my list on the refrigerator. We all need to do what works best for us.

I want to acknowledge my son, **David William Rask,** who has made me very proud to be his mom—especially after many years of uphill challenges. I thank God that you finally listened, matured, and took charge of your life to become independent and successful. I always said, "You could do and have whatever you want, along with living an obedient lifestyle."

As far as customer service is concerned, I want to let all of you know that the staff of AuthorHouse is in the business of providing exemplary service. **Thank you, AuthorHouse.** Your staff continues to be a pleasure to work with.

Until this day, I thank my mom, **Bernadette Murphy Neal,** who taught me at an early age to be responsible, hard-working, organized, and to have great work ethics. I also want to thank my grandparents, **Maria and Peter Kolisnik,** along with my aunt, **Resi Hofmann** for raising me to become responsible. I believe all parents and guardians need to teach their children these qualities. Many agree with me on this. I hope the rest of you who read this also agree!

"I'M ONLY A PENCIL IN THE EYES OF GOD, BUT IT IS HE WHO WRITES."
(Mother Teresa)

WORK ETHICS TODAY & THE GENERATION GAP!

(OPINIONS AND OBSERVATIONS)

What has happened to today's workforce and work ethics? Many students and adults seem to be lacking work ethics and responsibility. How can we change this and how do we get our families back together?

Today's students will be our teachers and leaders in the future!

Today's youth are too busy being "kids," talking on their cell phones, having sex, playing video games, playing on the Internet, hanging out, fighting, smoking, doing drugs, etc. Are they taking too many academic courses in school to be prepared for the work world? Maybe they are just too distracted or not motivated and they have too much time on their hands. Genetics may play a major part in today's kids.

What are work ethics? One customer said, "It was an oxymoron." An oxymoron is like jumbo shrimp, airline food, military intelligence, or family vacations.

Ethics has different meanings to different people. It usually involves learning what is right or wrong, then doing what is right. Some basic ethics include integrity, responsibility, loyalty, empathy, confidentiality, honesty, and respect.

So, have today's ethics and this generation changed or are we all just getting older and need to learn to adjust?

"Do the right thing. It will gratify some people and astonish the rest."
(Mark Twain)

He also notes the difficulty people have in accepting responsibility. "It's curious that physical courage is so common and moral courage is so rare."

Please know that we have many students and adults out in the workforce who are very responsible, doing well, and are successful. We are very proud of them. But there are not as many as in the past, and should we be considering the huge, diverse population we have?

Today's workforce is becoming a major concern with many businesses. Employers have a huge turnaround and constantly have to hire new employees because the ones they have are not reliable. This takes copious amounts of time and money. I have been putting people to work for twenty years, and employers and I share many of the same concerns.

Our present generation seems to be lacking the basics most of us grew up with, **"the soft skills,"** such as how to dress professionally, how to communicate, including on the telephone, how to interview, positive attitudes, etc.

I personally believe that most of today's generation lacks values. When many of us grew up in the 1960s or earlier, we were raised differently. We did not have all the toys and amenities today's children are given so freely. Everything we did have we had to work very hard for. Many things we just had to live without because our parents could not afford them. I know some of us who were less fortunate want to give our children more than what we had. That is great, however they still need to be shown value and appreciation. Kids today have an "owe me" mentality. Not long ago, I gave a high school graduate a computer monitor and keyboard. I did not expect lifelong gratitude, but she did not even say "thank you." It is amazing how many young adults I have sent wedding and baby gift certificates to who never said "thank you." When my son was living at home, he had a friend who would come over. Every time I gave him something, he would never say "thank you." So I began saying "You are welcome." Pretty soon he began saying "thank you." What happened to manners? I must say I am impressed when I encounter a student and he says, "yes, ma'am" or "thank you, ma'am." Too often all we hear is vulgarity and ungratefulness.

Some of us had parents who gave us an allowance every week to do the chores. Many of us passed on the same set of values and responsibilities to our children. When my son was younger, I always kept a chore board on the refrigerator. Now I use it for myself. Many of our children are now responsible and able to live and manage on their own. I would think all of us, as parents, want to see our kids happy, educated, successful, and independent enough to live on their own. **Our kids need positive role models**. Even if parents don't work or can't, they can still encourage their kids to go to school, do their homework, chores, and teach them to be responsible. It is difficult if parents don't have work ethics themselves. As a result of this, parents are unable to model golden standards for working to their children. We have so many young teenagers today who *are* parents. What are they teaching their kids? What many young people do not realize is this becomes a tradition, and then a legacy.

> **"Try not to become a person of success, but rather a person of value."**
> **(Albert Einstein)**

Many adults today are on some kind of unwarranted government assistance. There are, however, people who have no choice and really do need the financial help. However, many abuse the system and would just rather stay home to collect their money, as opposed to going out and working for a living. I can just imagine how many of us would enjoy that. Many parents give their kids everything they want. So where is the incentive for them to work? I had a seventeen-year-old student who told me he gets a weekly allowance but does not have to do any chores. He blamed it on his parents. (Bingo.) We are all here for a reason, not just to take up space and oxygen. Some only want to barely get by and have no higher goals or expectations of themselves. That makes it difficult for children living in that environment. I know cultures are different too. Some believe the woman's place is in the home. Some parents don't want their children to work. These parents want the older sons and daughters home and helping out with raising the younger siblings and doing chores. There are some parents who want their children to work just so they can contribute to the family income. I have worked with many students who have to give their paychecks to their parents. This may often detour children from working. This also makes it very difficult for the young adult to leave the nest and start a life completely on his own.

I went on a blind date last year with a gentleman who was in his forties still lived at home. Now, you can read into that whatever you like! At least he had a job. I remember a time after I got divorced and had a man move in with me. Obviously, I was still young and naïve. I owned a home at the time and worked full time. He was in the construction field. After a while, he decided to quit his job. This did not sit well with me, especially working as hard as I was working. Nine weeks later, I kicked him out. I am sure he thought he could just take advantage of me. My son was proud that I wised up too! There are men and women who will take advantage of those of us who work hard for a living. Unfortunately, caring people allow this to happen. Therefore, we all must be on guard.

One of life's challenges that our younger generation does not realize is that it is very tough and costly to live out on your own. When I was growing up and first began working, minimum wage was $3.25, then $3.65, then $4.25, and it stayed there for a long time. When President Clinton was in office, I actually wrote him a letter requesting he increase the minimum wage. In time, the beginning wage went to $5.25. In 2007, minimum wage went to $7.50 and will go to $8.00 per hour in the year 2008. Many do not realize that when minimum wage goes up, so does everything else. Sometimes this also detours businesses from hiring more applicants. Without a good job and income, it is very difficult to survive on your own, if not impossible. It takes many people working two jobs or having roommates just to pay the bills. When teens are living at home, the parents are supporting them and paying **all** the bills. They really will not understand what all it takes until they actually get out on their own. When I am working with teens, I always suggest to them to get a job while they are still at home and save their money to move out. **I believe we as parents** need to educate, help, and prepare our kids for their future as much as possible. It is even more critical now as the price of food, housing, and other living expenses keeps rising.

On a personal note, many of us don't believe it is fair that sports players, models, and actors make more money than those of us who work six to seven days a week in laborious jobs trying to make ends meet and make a difference, while others get paid for having fun, being beautiful and talented. (Such is life.) Raising the minimum wage does not make much of a difference if everything else goes up at the same time. This world seems so upside-down.

There was an article published in a high desert newspaper in July 2006 on income required to purchase a home today. It stated that the cost of the average home in the year 2006 is $325,000, with 5 percent down and a 6.8 percent interest rate. These figures mean the average household needs to make $75,000 a year or more. I can attest to that. I began looking for a home again in the summer of 2006. My payments on a $300,000 home would be $2,000 a month or more depending on the type of loan. I work two full-time jobs and I can't afford a house at that price. So how will others? An average rent payment for a two- to three-bedroom apartment in the year 2000 was about $500 a month. Now it is $950 to $1,600 a month. How are our graduates going to be able to live on their own? This could put us right back into a depression. Many are and will be losing their homes. Perhaps the military will be their best option. When I was married, we bought a brand-new home in the late '80s that had three bedrooms, two baths, and was on a quarter acre for $79,000. Later, when we divorced, I bought a three-bedroom, two-bath home for $82,000 in the mid '90s. That home today costs $300,000. This is totally unbelievable. Our children had better get serious about getting an education and good jobs.

Somewhere along the line, things changed and the lack of ethics is almost becoming an epidemic. Our school campuses never used to look the way some do now. When I was in school, littering was just not tolerated and discipline was always more severely enforced.

Trash cans are in place for a reason, yet students feel they can just drop their trash anywhere. When students get into trouble at school, maybe they should have them clean the campus instead of locking them in a classroom for a period doing nothing. Along with getting suspended from school for doing wrong, we had harder punishment at home when we broke the rules. When I went to school in the '60s and did something wrong in class or did not know the answer to a problem, I was slapped on the hand with a ruler and or put in a corner on my knees for a while. That was very humiliating. When I came home and did wrong, I was put on a very rough carpet on my knees until it hurt. Until this day, I can't be on my knees very long before they begin to hurt. When I returned to live with my mom in the early '70s and did wrong, I was beaten with a belt. Let me tell you, that hurt. When I used bad language, my mouth was washed out with soap. The way our kids use foul language today, we would probably run out of soap. If I stole something, I was threatened to have my fingers burned off. It sure made me think twice. Nowadays, if we do that to our children, we can go to jail. It is important to give our children unconditional love; however, we also need to give them rules to live by. Even

God in the King James Version of the Bible said, "Discipline your son and honor your mother and father."

When my son was growing up and he did wrong, as much as it hurt me, I did not think twice about smacking him, especially if he smart-mouthed to me. Why do we change the things that work? When I was younger and saw parents spoiling their kids who cried until they got what they wanted, I knew they would grow up being greedy and not appreciating things.

Today's generation does not seem to understand how fortunate they are to have what they have and the opportunities that are available to them. I think in the overall population, the more we get, the more we want, and we don't seem to be satisfied. There are always new things coming out that are bigger and better. Everyone wants to keep up with the Joneses due to prestige and peer pressure. We are living in an instant-gratification society when it comes to satisfying our wants and needs. "Got to have it now." Most of us don't realize the material stuff is temporary and we can't take it with us when we die. Take a look at a junk yard; you can bet that those old and smashed cars were all someone's dream cars at one time.

"The art of living a happy life lies not in having more of what you want but in getting better at enjoying what you have." (Michael Josephson)

Kids today can't relate to black-and-white TV or listening to radio. I grew up when there were no phones and we had to go to the post office to use the payphone. We had three basic channels on TV. I remember going to the bathroom outside in an outhouse and wearing the same clothes for days. Years ago, there were no computers, e-mails or cell phones, and we managed just fine.

"It has been clear that our technology has suppressed our humanity." (Albert Einstein)

It has been said, "Back in the '40s, grass was something we mowed not smoked. Aids were teachers, and principal's assistants. Coke was something we drank not put up our nose. Pot was something we cooked in not inhaled. Closets were for clothes, not coming out of, and people got married first then lived together." My, how times have changed; it does sound like a generation gap.

In class, students always have their cell phones on, either retrieving messages or text messaging when they think no one is watching. I call students often on their cell phones, hoping to leave a message; however, most of them answer their phones while they are in class. I tell them that it's not appropriate, and they should let it go to voice mail. Many times, calling students on their cell phones is the only way to reach them, especially when no one at home speaks English. I do not understand how someone can live in America and not speak English. When I came to this country, I learned English in two weeks. In Europe it is mandatory in school to learn English. In the spring of 2007, teachers were made to take an EL/Clad certification class to work with English learners. Even our education system and government are enabling our generation to do nothing! I believe we need more parenting classes because not all parents know how to be a parent. Especially our youth who are parents.

We did just fine without cell phones in school, and we concentrated more. Cell phones are a huge distraction, to the point where students leave the classroom to talk on the phone. Often, students have very offensive voice answering machines and probably will not be getting interview calls. Even we as adults have cell phones, and when we are in meetings, they ring and cause a huge distraction. It is really sad when you go to the restroom in public places and have to be on your cell phone. I am sorry, but I do not want to be that important. People often ask me why I have a cell phone if it is never turned on. My response is, "I have voice mail and believe it is very rude and distracting to have phones ring in meetings, church, etc." Granted, there are times when they need to be on, but at certain times they need to be on vibrate or off. Look at all the car accidents being caused by people on their phones and not paying attention. One student told me she can't live without her cell phone. One day she went to school and forgot her phone, so she went back home to get it. In summer of 2007, I ran into a customer at a local grocery store who had her young daughter in one of those push cars while talking on the cell phone. As she walked by me, she said, "I have to train her early talking on the phone while driving." I just laughed; I am sure you can imagine what I was thinking.

> **"Don't allow the phone to interrupt important moments. It's there for your convenience, not the caller's."**
> **(H. Jackson Brown, Jr.)**

It seems like before the world became full of commodities, life was simpler. Back then, families actually ate meals together, talked to each other, and knew what was going on in each other's lives. We need to learn to listen, spend time with our kids, and not just allow the television to be their babysitter. Some kids are watching television, on the Internet, or playing video games about thirty-five to fifty-five hours a week. For many, that time could be a full-time job. We all know the Internet is wonderful to an extent. But for many of our kids and even adults, it is doing more harm than good, especially when it comes to sex and pornography. Maybe the computers need to be in the family rooms and have computer protection software installed so parents can monitor what their children are doing. Even parents say that children are online way too much.

When our kids go to the movies, we should ask what they are seeing. My son came to me a couple of times asking me if he could go to a party. I would immediately ask, "What kind of party, where is it, who is the parent, and what is the phone number?" Then he would not tell me and he would not go. At least not to my knowledge. To me as a parent, these are very important questions to ask. What if I had let him go and he did not come home? I would be driving myself insane wondering where he was and what might have happened to him. Do most parents really know what goes on at some of these parties? I had a friend who let her son who was under the age of eighteen go to a party and he ended up with alcohol poisoning and in the hospital. The bottom line is we need to invest time in our kids because they grow up way too fast. You might consider holding a family rally once a week or scheduling dates with your spouse and kids.

I am happy to see that there are some commercials now about **"the family table"** sharing more than just meals together. Hopefully this will be an inspiration to all of us. We may need some type of teen rescue plan. Either way, we all need to get involved, especially those who don't work or need something to do. Consider the difference we could make.

> **"I am only one; but still I am one. I cannot do everything, but still I can do something. I will not refuse to do the something I can do."**
> **(Helen Keller)**

Lifestyles have changed drastically. Many parents are working hours away from their homes and don't get home until early or even late evenings. This means many kids are alone at home or on the streets. Single or divorced parents means a single parent is often left working two jobs and raising her kids. Many have to work, and sometimes more than one job. That makes it difficult to be a part of the children's lives. I can attest to that, because when I became a single parent, I had to work two full-time jobs. When I say, "had to," it was a choice. I could have chosen welfare or to live and barely get by. However, I wanted more for my son and me. My son was originally a very responsible, disciplined child until he was at home more than I was. That changed his life very quickly. This made my life a living nightmare, and I lost almost everything trying to save him, because a drug ring had moved in next door. I walked away from my home and everything I had invested in it in order to save my son. It was a sacrifice I chose. It was only by the grace of God that we got through the rough times because the values were rooted in him. Now he can be a testimony for others.

Those of us who are parents remember the terrible twos, threes, etc. Well, I believe our kids also go through the terrible teens; they develop an attitude. I vaguely remember when I turned thirteen that my attitude and emotions changed, especially being a girl. I am sure my mom can attest to that. Just like we learn to walk and talk, we go through changes as we grow. Now I call them "senior moments." There were times I just could not figure out or reason with my son, no matter what I said or did. I often wondered where that great honor-roll child disappeared to. It is almost like he had split in two or developed dissociative identity disorder. One day my son David said to me, "Mom, you just don't understand what it is like to be sixteen." I would just laugh and then say, "No, son I have no idea what it is like to be sixteen. I just woke up one day and was thirty-five! However, you have no idea what it is like to be my age." Then of course, there was no response, and he would just walk off.

Values, responsibilities, and work ethics really need to begin at home and at an early age. Our youth today is even more influential than in the past. They end up becoming what and whom they hang around with. Some of us were the same when we were younger. We got into trouble too, usually for ditching school or smoking in the bathrooms. Nothing as severe as what goes on today. However, the values were still there. We just needed people to care and not give up on us, which should be no different today. We need to make our children accountable, especially with gangs, terrorism, and the music to which they listen to. I do not even call most of that music. Do parents actually sit down and listen to the vulgarity, sex, drugs, violence, etc. that is in those lyrics? It seems like we are purposely destroying our kids.

Schools today sure have changed drastically. When I went to school, there was no such thing as home school, charter schools, or other options for youth. It seems now more than ever, students are leaving school for various different reasons. Most of it has to do with gangs, bringing weapons to school, being threatened, peer pressure, too many students, and not feeling safe or comfortable. Some are even being taken out because they are failing too many classes, and some just quit. It makes it difficult to learn with all the peer pressure and not feeling safe. School is stressful enough with all the different types of tests and the California High School Exit Exam. When kids drop out of school and later decide to get their GED, it is usually harder and there is often a waiting list. It is also more difficult to obtain employment.

I had to take my son out of school the end of his junior year for similar reasons. It was not fair to his education. Enrolling him in a school where he only went two days a week to turn in his homework was a joke. I made a secret drive by our neighborhood one day when he should have been inside studying. Before lunch, I found him strolling around the block with several other kids who were also on home schooling. We immediately discontinued that education. This home schooling just allows many to have more free time on their hands and get into trouble, especially when parents are not home with them.

I believe our education system needs to change drastically. Our students need discipline, and some of our schools could greatly benefit from having military leaders to run them. Some reasons there are so many dropouts are as follows:

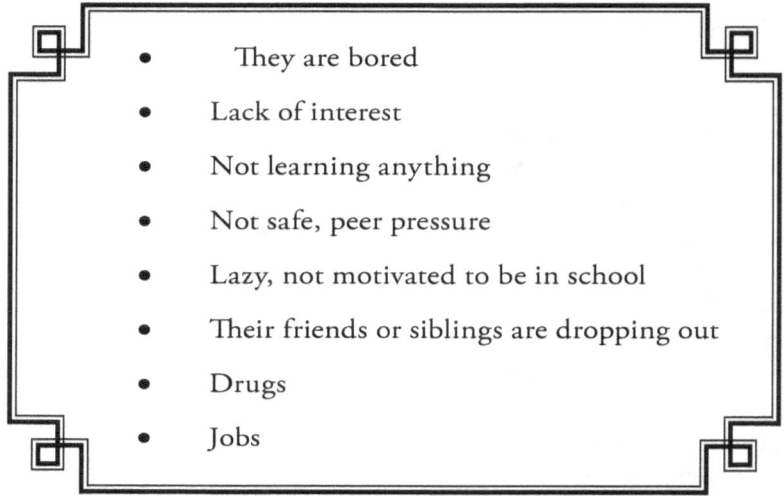

- They are bored
- Lack of interest
- Not learning anything
- Not safe, peer pressure
- Lazy, not motivated to be in school
- Their friends or siblings are dropping out
- Drugs
- Jobs

Many students are falling through the cracks or may have given up hope. So what do these kids do when they drop out? I am sure many of us know the answer to that. For some students, there seems to be a cycle of low or no expectations. As we know, we all fall and rise to expectations. Schools are not the same in each state. Some schools are very plush and have all the modern technologies. Others are run down and need serious renovations. Some of those schools are like small communities in a poor/low-income neighborhood. We need to find new ways to motivate our students along with staying motivated ourselves so we don't reach burnout. The '50s were called the Industrial Age, and now we are in the Technological Age. Some students have stated in some of the communities, the schools don't prepare them for any college, let alone the Ivy League campuses.

The education system in Europe is completely different. Students actually have a trade when they exit school. Obviously, our world has changed drastically, yet most of the education system has not. I believe our teachers need to be retrained. Doctors and dentists continually go to school and take classes to keep up with the current and future medicines, treatments, technologies, etc. Since we know our present and future students will be our leaders tomorrow, we need to change our education system with a new mindset and a new plan. I strongly believe those of us who are teachers need to demonstrate the relevance to the real world to each subject we are teaching. For example, if we are teaching math, we need to show our students how to write checks and balance a checkbook, how to open a savings and checking account, how to budget, and give back change or money. Most of our students have no clue what a W-4 or W-2 is. When they apply for jobs, they have difficulties filling out the W-4, including job applications. I believe everything we teach, we need to show our students how it will apply to their lives. Even taking a shorthand class can help them get a job as a court stenographer making $80,000 a year. We need to encourage and mandate classes for students to take that will give them the hands-on experience for their independence and careers. There are teachers who are doing this, but I believe we all need to do this to help our future leaders of tomorrow. **We as parents need to do this**. We need to show our children what an electric bill looks like and costs and how much they may need to earn to live on their own.

Many of our current college students may have heard the name Martin Luther King, Jr. and know they get the day off. However, many have no clue about his speech, "I have a dream," and what it represents.

"It is not enough to be a hard-working person. We must consider what are we working at? What are we working towards."
(Martin Luther King Jr.)

Should algebra be mandatory? Or should it go back to being an elective? When I went to school, algebra was an elective. To this day, I have no use for algebra. Our students are taking so many required classes that there is little room for vocational classes that will help them obtain a job or career. I wish I would have learned in school how to purchase a car, a home, fill out a credit application, how to budget, make investments, etc. Instead, I learned it all the hard way, with many mistakes and unwise choices. It is amazing how many high-school graduates can't read. How will they be able to complete a job application?

When I was going to school, I remember my fifth-grade teacher, Mrs. Tomaya; she always dressed in suits and was very professional. Mr. Dolan, my ninth-grade science teacher, almost always wore a tie. To me, they were role models. I always dress up everywhere I go, especially in the classroom. How would it look if I showed up in sweats or jeans and told my students how to apply for a job? I have gone into classrooms where there were teachers with their feet up on their desks, reading a newspaper, and some with their sunglasses on. Most teachers today are much more casual than when I was growing up. So what happened to professionalism? I strongly believe if we want to be taken seriously, we need to look and act as the professionals we are. Even Bill Gates has stated, "I am terrified of tomorrow's workforce."

See Web site: Standup.org. The Bill & Melinda Gates Foundation.

Schools now have changed many of their vending machines from soda machines to juice machines. Many of the juices contain as much sugar as sodas. We need to add fruit and healthy energy bars to the vending machines. Just like our cars need good fuel to run, so do our bodies. It is important for our students to get healthy nourishment, especially in the mornings. Due to early school schedules, many students don't have time to eat breakfast, and often it is just too early to eat.

If students are not emotionally ready to go to work, it would be better for them to wait until they are. They burn many bridges along the way. What many of them don't realize is that when they don't show up for work, quit, or are terminated, they will not have a good reference for the next job for which they apply. Many of them quit because they don't like the job, it is too hard, or it is not what they thought it would be. It would be so much better if they just gave the employer two weeks' notice and said, "Sorry, I am giving my notice because this job is not for me." Employers count on people to be there, and when the employees do not show up, the company is short-handed, meaning someone else has to do their job. Hence, sometimes, the long lines or lack of customer service.

> **"Everything we do is just a drop in the ocean, but without that drop, it is missing forever."**
> **(Mother Teresa)**

There is no

such thing

as failure

if you try.

But what if I try

and don't succeed?

What do you call that?

Learning!

(Anonymous)

EXAMPLE OF THE GERMAN SCHOOL SYSTEM

Schools in Germany: From the age of six through fourteen, school is mandatory and the public state-run schools are free. The school system in Germany is a little different from its American counterpart. All children enter in the same program, but at the age of ten, they go to one of four types of schools. The track that they enter determines which type of school they can attend next, and finally, whether they will go to a university or train for a technical field or trade.

Kindergarten (literally translated: a garden or yard for kids) is not a part of the regular public school system, and is not required or free. Tuition is normally based on income. Even though it's not mandatory, more than 67 percent of three- to six-year-olds attend. Many more children would attend if it weren't for the limited space. The kindergartens are usually run by churches, organizations, and private companies.

From the age of six through nine, all children must attend **Grundschule or primary school (Pronounced - Groond shoe-lay).** Teachers recommend their students to a particular school based on academic achievement and self-confidence to work independently. Here one teacher will teach them the basic skills like reading, writing, and math and religion. They also have a class called "*Heimat* and *Sachunterricht*" which is where they learn about local history, geography, and biology. In addition to their base teacher, they go to separate teachers for music and P.E.

This is also the time where children are evaluated for the next level of schooling. In the fifth and sixth grades (the "orientation grades"), the decision is made which track the student will go to next, based on the student's ability, speed of learning, intelligence, and the goals of students and their families.

The lowest track in the German education system is the **Hauptschule (general school). (pronounced – How-pt-shoelay)** It starts with fifth grade and goes up through the ninth grade. A *Hauptschule* is a school where the students prepare for occupations that require less training. They also continue learning basic subjects as well as English. After a student graduates from a *Hauptschule,* he or she can go to a vocational school, which last about two years. This is a school that will teach them to become blue-collar workers (mechanics) or grocery-store employees. This school may also petition for students to advance to a *Realschule*.

A **Realschule (pronounced – Ree-al-shoelay)** is a school that's a little more advanced than the *Hauptschule*. In most counties, this school goes from fifth to tenth grade. Here, students learn the basic subjects, which will prepare them for a mid-level job in business. In a *Realschule*, it's possible (if students receive high enough grades) to transfer to a *Gymnasium*. **An employer friend of mine became a medical assistant through this school.** It is a privilege to attend the *Realschule* and the *Gymnasium*.

The **Gymnasium (pronounced – Gim-nauseum)** is one of the tracks a student could go to after primary school. This school, which prepares students to enter a university, goes for eight years, from fifth through thirteenth grades. Here, students learn subjects like German, math, physics, chemistry, geography, biology, art, P.E., religion, and history. They are also required to learn two foreign languages. (One has to be English.) In the thirteenth grade, students prepare for the *Abitur*, a comprehensive examination that students must pass in order to go on to a university.

A **Gesamtschule (comprehensive school) (pronounced – Gay-sompt-shoelay)** combines the *Gymnasium*, the *Realschule*, and the *Hauptschule*. This type of school was first introduced in Germany in the '60s and has been controversial ever since. Scholars have debated whether students can learn better in this type of environment. A student at a comprehensive school can switch between the different tracks without changing buildings.

The Abitur (pronounced ab-eh-tour) is a crucial examination that German students take to get into a university. They take this week long test at the end of their thirteenth year. Because this test is so important, the school closes down the part of the school where the thirteenth grade is taking the *Abitur*, and the quiet of the halls is strictly enforced. Students who pass the *Abitur* receive a maturity certificate that allows them into a university. If they fail, they only have a few more chances to pass or they won't be allowed to attend a university.

In Germany, as in the United States, public education is the responsibility of each (sixteen state counties/*Bundeslander*). Therefore, the German school system and types of schools vary from state to state. Not all of the schools listed will be found in every *Bundesland*. In Austria, the school system is a federal responsibility and much more centralized than in Germany and Switzerland. Like in the U.S. and Britain, Germany has compulsory school attendance. *(Schulpflicht)* rather than compulsory education. As a result, home schooling is not permitted. By law (since 1871), young people between the ages of six and fourteen must attend school. German public education is free, including university study. (Although there is no tuition cost, German university students must pay for books and living expenses.)

German students usually attend a *Grundschule* (*Volksschule* in Austria) for the first four years (kindergarten is not mandatory, nor is it usually part of the public school system). At the age of ten in most *Bundeslanders,* students and their parents must decide the next step in their education. That is, which type of school they will attend: *Hauptschule, Realschule,* or *Gymnasium* (in that order of prestige and difficulty).

The German education system is different in many ways from the ones in Anglo-Saxon countries, and it produces high-performing students. Although education is a function of the federal states, and there are differences from state to state, some generalizations are possible.

Efforts have been made in the postwar years to make the system more democratic, though some feel that the changes don't go far enough. It's nevertheless possible for a child with the right academic ability to study right up to the university level, regardless of the financial status of the family.

One of the reforms concluded that if a student's track is decided too early, after completion of the fourth grade, a child could bound for the universities, and hence for the more prestigious and better-paying careers. This rule has been modified somewhat, and it is theoretically possible for a high-achieving student to get back on the university track at a later stage, although this is not a frequent occurrence.

Renate's Story:

My name is Renate; I grew up in Germany and progressed through the German school system. I married an American and immigrated to America when I was eighteen years old.

My school experience started with attending *Gurndschule* for five years. I was recommended by my teachers to transfer to the *Mittelschule* (pronounced Middle-shoe-lay) due to my good grades. I attended an "all-girl" school until I graduated. During my second year, I had some teenage moments and my grades dropped. The principal consulted with my parents and actually recommended me to be moved back to *Grundschule* because I was not applying myself. (It is a privilege to be asked by educators to attend the *Mittelschule* and/or *Gymnasium*.) You can be moved back at any time to the *Grundschule* if the students do not perform the way they should. I was allowed to stay, repeat the class, and finally graduate.

After graduation, I wanted to learn the profession of medical technologist. I applied at a school, but was not accepted. The government in Germany is very strict. They do not allow a young person to just sit at home. After the school rejected my application, my parents needed to report to the government agency to find out what my future goals were. The government agency then sent a letter to my parents that I had to attend a home economics school for one year. This is where we learned cooking, sewing, parenting, typing, work ethics, etc. During this time, I decided to become a medical assistant. At the age of sixteen, I had to find a physician who would hire me as a *"Lehrling"* (apprentice) for a small salary, and in addition provide me with the clinical time that was needed. It took almost fifteen different office visits before I found a physician who would accommodate my needs.

I then had to enroll into a technical school for didactic education one day a week. I learned the paperwork, the laws, some office procedures, and the rest of the week I worked at the physician's office. I was able to find a position in a urology praxis (physician's office). This particular office had an X-ray laboratory and examination room set up. During my two years of education, I learned front office and laboratory procedures, including how to manage a physician's office. After two years, I had to pass the state test to obtain my medical assistant's certificate. Two months after my state test, I went to America and continued my education and career. **Today, I am a registered nurse and actively working in the healthcare profession.**

CUSTOMER SERVICE

CHAPTER TWO

"**The customer is always right.**" Where have we heard that before? These are words that were first spoken by hotel impresario/hotelier César Ritz.

César Ritz was born in 1852, and was a Swiss peasant with an education that never took him past simple mathematics. He started out as a waiter at the age of sixteen and was fired four times. An employer told him that he did not have the flair/style that was needed for the hotel business. However, perseverance kept him going.

He later obtained a job in a premier Paris restaurant. He became an expert at observing how things were done and learned a great deal. Later he left and began managing different restaurants in European resorts. Ritz often said if a guest did not like the entrée, it was immediately taken from the table. If a customer complained about the bill, César took it and "forgot" to return it. He did what it took to please his guests.

In 1892, he went to London to save a hotel from financial destruction. He redecorated the bridal suite and became upset by the way the light was shining from a brass chandelier. So he put lamps behind two protruding cornices for a more romantic setting. This is then how indirect lighting was born. He wanted to have the soft lighting flatter women's faces and gowns. One time he smelled soap on a glass in the dining room. He had all three hundred rewashed. He remade beds to make sure they were perfect. He was the first to provide dinner music with the Johann Strauss Orchestra.

Before he passed away in 1918, he built a grand hotel at Place Vendome in Paris. Thus began a plethora/conglomerate of exclusive hotels all over bearing his name, known today as **The Ritz-Carlton.**

His wife Marie continued the expansion of hotels bearing his name. The legacy endured with his son Charles Ritz, who passed away in 1977. The hotels and rights were later sold to William B. Johnson, who established the Ritz-Carlton Hotel Company. The Marriott International purchased 49 percent interest in the Ritz-Carlton in 1995. After three years, it was increased to 99 percent. César Ritz designed the lion crown logo. It is a combination of the British royal seal (the crown) and the lion, the logo of a financial backer.

> **"I'm not here just to make a living; I'm here to make a difference."**
> **(Helice Bridges)**

I was at a ninety-nine-cent retail store one day, and there were two cashiers and very long lines. Being a job developer, I asked the cashier if they were in need of help. She said, "No we have plenty of employees; they just decided not to come to work today."

Customer service is not the way it used to be and not the same everywhere. Customer service also has a great deal to do with our new generation working in those jobs. One of the grocery stores that I visit weekly always has new courtesy clerks. I tell my job seekers all the time that this particular store hires every week, but I never see any of them working there. One day when I was at this store, I asked the courtesy clerk to please double paper bag my order. Shortly afterwards, I had to ask him again because he did not do it. Then the cashier also asked him. By the time I got home, none of my order was double bagged. Did he not understand, was he not listening, or did he just not care? How many times have you come home from the grocery store and found your eggs and bread on the bottom? How many times have you been missing parts of your order? The cashiers have told me that this happens regularly. I am impressed when some of the cashiers see me coming and they immediately tell the courtesy clerks to double paper bag my order. That is great customer service!

My friends know that I have a favorite store where I like to shop. I like this store because they have a variety of clothes and gifts. They have my sizes and great prices. They usually provide background music for a more pleasurable shopping experience. It is a wonderful store, however word got around that it was a great place for bargains, including myself as a walking advertisement.

I have noticed in the past three years that the store has become more and more uninviting. On occasions I have walked in and walked out without making a purchase. It's mostly due to the customers trashing the store. They allow their children to run through the store and underneath the racks. The clothes end up on the floor. That is merchandise that does not sell. Clothes are often not in the right size category because people just put the merchandise anywhere. There are often men's and baby clothes in the women's dress section.

Many businesses only have so many hours they divide with their staff. When a business closes, there are many duties that need to be performed, including cleaning and picking up after us customers. When I am in the store going through the racks and a dress falls off the hanger, I pick it up and put it back. I find myself often picking clothing off the floor and putting things on the end of the rack. Call me odd, but I have gone as far as when I see a matching outfit that is missing a piece and come across the other half, I put the two together. It is often frustrating when you find something and the other half is missing.

There are businesses that have really poor customer service and people don't return. If you had a business, would you not want to know why? There was this restaurant in town that was always very slow at getting our meals to us. Many of us had one-hour lunch periods, and by the time we got our lunch, it would be time to go. I wrote the manager a letter, informing them that I really enjoyed their food but their service was too slow. It was at least six months before I returned to that restaurant. After we ordered, it only took ten minutes to receive our meals. I sent the manager a thank-you card and we have had prompt service ever since. When I go to a business and receive excellent customer service, I also send a thank-you letter to let the business know. Either way, if it were my business, I would want to know so that I can make improvements or maybe reward my employees. Often, things can't be changed if you are not aware of the problem. Many complain about certain issues but then don't want to do anything to change it. I encourage people to write letters to their legislators, city officials, town mayors, etc. When I drive the same route daily at an intersection where there are many accidents and no signal lights, I write a letter. Sometimes it changes, sometimes it doesn't.

We as customers can be rude and demanding at times, depending on with whom we are dealing and what our day has been like. We all know, "customers come first!"

I am very impressed with businesses that acknowledge you or welcome you as soon as you walk in, especially when they are busy assisting others. There are times when employees call out sick and the company is short-handed. Sometimes there may only be one person working, and then several people walk in all needing service. We have all been there, and some on both sides. It is not the fault of the one person who is left at the register with several people in line. This puts a great deal of stress on that person. I remember when I worked in the meat department of a grocery store and they would send people home at night when it was slow. Sure enough, when everyone left, I always got busy and had many frustrated customers. We need to keep in mind that without customers or guests, we have no business.

Let's take the post office, banks, and grocery stores as an example. How many times have we stood in those lines thinking, *they have all these windows and check stands but only two to four open?* So, where lies the blame and how do we change this monotony? When I worked in retail and we did not carry something a customer needed, I made recommendations on who did and the customers appreciated it. If you provide good customer service, then people will return. One of the last times I used a pest-control service, they told me that I had a ninety-day guarantee. If the pests returned, they would come back and spray free of charge. After the first two weeks, the pests returned, including new ones. I called and called the pest-control company. They never returned my calls and never came out to fix the problem. I reported them to the Better Business Bureau and they did nothing! What type of customer service do we call this?

In the summer of 2006, I began looking for a home again, so I had to get a lender and loan approval. The loan consultant then told me that I qualify for a three hundred- to four hundred thousand-dollar home. When I found a home for $289,000, he wrote up a good-faith estimate, and my payments would have been $2,000.00 a month. I told him I could not go past $1,500.00 a month. He told me then I need to look at homes that are $240,000 and under. My Realtor and I then began looking in that price range, which was very difficult due to my meticulous needs and the high prices. Most of the homes we looked at were trashed. When I walked away from my home, I made sure it was clean! It is amazing how some people live. After weeks and months passed, the loan consultant told us of new programs that would bring my payments down and then told us we can start looking in the $270,000 price range. We finally put in a couple of offers. In the meantime, every time we spoke with the loan consultant, he had a different answer for us as far as what the monthly payments would be. Finally we found a great house for $269,000. We made the offer, it was accepted, and we were in escrow. The loan consultant ordered the appraisal and the home inspection was done. Escrow was to close Thanksgiving weekend. I was told to start packing. Since I work so many jobs and have so many responsibilities, I was working around the clock to get packed and make arrangements so I could be in by the holidays. Two weeks after escrow, the loan consultant told us he couldn't do the loan. Needless to say, we were all stressed out and very disappointed. I told the loan consultant I would come by the next day on my lunch hour to collect my original personal paperwork. He told me I needed to give him a check for two credit reports. I had already given him one when we began the loan process. Before I went to his office, he left me several messages that I needed to also write him a $350 check for the appraisal. My Realtor said I did not need to do that. When I went to his office to request my paperwork, he would not give it to me until I wrote him a check. He began arguing with me and I began hyperventilating to where I almost passed out. I told him this whole ordeal had made me ill for the past three weeks. Now I have no house, no loan, my house is all packed; my mom and I got into an argument over this because she told me I was being set up for disappointment. He finally gave me some of my paperwork. Later that afternoon, I passed out at work due to all the stress he had been putting me through. The next day he sent me an e-mail that if I did not send him the money for the appraisal, he would be most disappointed in his own misjudgment of my character. Unbelievable. After a week passed, I sent a letter to the loan consultant and the mortgage company that this was not a good customer-service experience for me. Of course, I never heard from either of them again.

I immediately found another loan officer, and he gave me some options, but the monthly payments would be too high and it would not be a fixed rate. He then basically told me I can't afford a house in that price range. So we were all led down the primrose path, including the seller. Since I did not know how long it would take to find another home in the new price range and did not want my son to come home for the holidays to everything in boxes, I began unpacking. I refuse to live in chaos, especially for the holidays. I believed that eventually I would find the right home. It is all a matter of patience and timing.

In the spring of 2007, I developed carpal tunnel from typing. My doctor prescribed Relafen for the pain. About three weeks later, I began feeling very strange with some side effects. When I went to see the doctor to discuss the situation, she told me I was supposed to take two a day, not two after each meal. The pharmacy typed the label wrong. These pills were each 750 mg. I was basically suffering from medication poisoning. When I went to the drug store to tell them about the mistake they had made, their response was, "Oh"; that was it. If I had not stopped the medication when I did, I may have died. I guess it was no big deal. I could have sued them. Mistakes happen, but some are deadly. I believe doctors should be made to type out their prescriptions, since their writing often cannot be understood.

Most businesses work off of referrals. How often do we refer people or our friends to places that have helped us? How many of us have said, "Don't go there"? Most of our best customers are our repeat customers. What happened to the personal touch? How many of us have spent thirty to sixty minutes on the telephone waiting to speak with a human? In 2007, I had to call one of my credit card companies regarding my bill. I never reached a human being. I was given several options on what numbers to press. The number zero was not an option. Every number I selected was another automated voice and it would not let me speak with a human. After several attempts, I was forced to write them a letter. I have spent numerous lunch hours only to get nowhere! Can anyone relate?

"Accountability: It's not only what we do, but also what we do not do for which we are accountable." (Moliére)

As far as working with the public, not all of us are comfortable working with others. That is why some people work behind the scenes, where there is not a lot of interaction with people. When I interview students and applicants, some of the questions I always ask are "What does good customer service mean to you, how would you treat an angry customer, and can you give me an example of a time when you received good customer service?"

I always get a variety of responses. Most of us know we should all treat people the way we would want to be treated.

It is not always enough to say "The customer comes first." We deal with very astute, informed buyers. Most customers know the difference between poor, mediocre, and excellent/exceptional service. It has been said many times, "Knowledge is power," but "The use of knowledge is much more powerful." It is important to train and empower the employees who serve on the front lines.

Rewarding or providing discounts for your repeat customers can be very profitable. You may refer your customers to other businesses and ask your customers to tell them by whom they were referred. It can be a win–win for all parties involved. Sometimes we may need to treat customers' problems or needs as if they were our own. That would make exceptional customer service. Other times being able to correct or advise a customer's dilemma can have a tremendous impact on the relationships you develop, including the return of your customers.

Does 100 percent guaranteed = customer satisfaction?

Does on time, every time = dependability?

There are many ways to provide exceptional customer service. I am not the expert, but talking to those who are would be a great start. Here are just a few examples to ponder.

Of course, I may be preaching to the choir!

- Talk to other businesses, observe what they are doing or not.

- Select a mystery shopper and go to other businesses, and or have one in your own business so you can evaluate your employees.

- Conduct surveys.

- Keep files on regular customers.

- Use comment cards.

- Try to remember people's names and faces.

- Set goals and make a business plan.

- Attend seminars and or, bring in professionals.

- Follow up and send thank-you cards or letters.

From Bob Sole, Express Blinds, Draperies & Shutters. A business owner's point of view on customer service and work ethics:

Communication, Communication, Communication!

- Customers would rather hear from you with not-so-good news or delays in your product or service than not hear from you at all.

- Make every waking moment as productive as possible both personally and professionally. It's all time management and the art of scheduling.

- Honesty is always the best policy even if the customer does not want to hear it.

- Don't be afraid to apologize and accept blame.

- Be a problem-solver; quit blaming others, and come up with solutions.

- Always try to return customers' phone calls in the same day or in a timely manner.

- Meet with staff regularly to discuss projects, ideas, suggestions, problems, solutions, and how to solve them expediently.

- Arrive early and work a little later when needed.

- Be a self-starter; employers do not have time to baby-sit.

- Some employees are not as productive as they could be; come up with ideas to contribute to the company/team.

- There is always something that can be done.

- Make a difference in your workplace, at home, and in your community and you will be rewarded tenfold.

I learned a long time ago from my friend Jim Veal to make somebody's day, throw him or her an unexpected compliment. Make someone feel special; it will be the best gift you can give.

—Dana Gordon, Author of *Success Tidbits and Real Estate Broker*

No matter where you go or what you do in business, there is a customer. Serving that customer is what the business of business is. Follow the Ritz-Carlton example.

As Bob Sole put it, "Communication, communication, communication." Always listen to your customers and don't assume anything. Say what you mean and mean what you say. Have integrity. When a customer or client has what they perceive as an objection or a complaint, it is essential to listen to the entire story. There may be a lot of information that seems irrelevant, but you need to wade through it all to find the real source of objection or dissatisfaction the customer or client is trying to express. Listening requires focus on what the other person is saying. That is why God gave us two ears and one mouth.

When people are working, they must feel they are part of something. This includes safety and a fair wage so they can provide for themselves and their families. As managers and employers, it is our job to provide these basic needs.

A few success tidbits:

- Always ask for help when you need it.

- Be committed, do what you say you will do.

- Keep an open mind, embrace change with open arms, and look for the opportunity to learn and grow.

- Affirmation, what you say is what you get.

- Writing your goals down causes your thoughts to be crystallized and focused.

- Be willing to go the extra mile.

- Customer service and more customer service.

- I'm a work addict.

- Continuous improvement, doing a little bit each day is an excellent way to learn a new habit or skill.

- The time decision and your responsibility, just as Robin states in her time-management section and book, "There are 24 hours in a day and 168 hours in a week. The common fib is, "I don't have time." We must set aside time blocks for family, self, and appointments. The next time you are asked to participate in anything, give the real answer not the time excuse.

- Believe, you must believe you can achieve the goal you have chosen.

- Give thanks always.

Rex Weissenbach / Owner of Big O Tires & Service Centers

The customer is always right, even if they are wrong, because of our failure to explain what we were trying to do for them in whatever product or service we are providing. In the service business and in life, if you are having a bad day, "be a good actor." Some people only like to bring people down instead of bringing them up. "Whatever business you are in, you are in the people business."

The Basic Functions of a Business:

- Need to plan, be organized, have a leader, and then control it. Then it starts all over again.

- Need to have humility and compassion. People want a fair price with good service.

- Objections are stepping-stones to sales.

- It's not the money, it's the journey.

- You must have passion for what you do or find another job.

I am inexpensive but I'm not cheap. As a businessman, I mean what I say and I say what I mean. "Only the best for you, I am a professional."

"Money is not that important, but it ranks right up there with oxygen."
(Zig Ziglar)

Tyson/A Repeat Customer of Big O Tires:

"If you have goals, you can do anything."

John Davison / Office Manager

Welfare has caused it to be easy due to our government. We have lost a generation. Parents are not spending quality time with their kids, even when they are with them. The problem of today's society and generation is mostly due to taking discipline and God out of the schools.

What you may not know about customer service:

More than a decade ago, the following was reported according to the White House Office of Consumer Affairs:

- The average business never hears from 96 percent of its unhappy customers.

- For every complaint received a business, will have twenty-six others that are not reported, six of them being "serious."

- Those "non-complaining" customers actually complain to about ten others.

- Complainers are most likely to do business again with companies where their complaints were not resolved versus non-complainers?

> **"Every customer is a guest in our store and should be treated as such."**
> **(Charles A. Walgreen, Sr.)**

"I Am Your Customer"

"I am your customer." Satisfy my wants, add personal attention, and a friendly touch, and I will become a walking advertisement for your products and services. Ignore my wants, show carelessness, inattention, and poor management, and I will simply cease to exist as far as you are concerned.

"I am sophisticated, much more so than I was a few years ago. My needs are more complex. I have grown accustomed to better things. I have money to spend.

"I am an egotist. I am sensitive; I am proud. My ego needs the nourishment of a friendly, personal greeting from you. It is important to me that you appreciate my business. After all, when I buy your products and services, my money is feeding you.

"I am a perfectionist. I want the best I can get for the money I spend. When I criticize your food, beverage, or service—and I will, to anyone who will listen—when I am dissatisfied, then take heed. The source of my discontent lies in something you or the products you serve have failed to do. Find that source and eliminate it, or you will lose my business and that of my friends as well.

"I am fickle. Other businessmen continually beckon to me with offers of more for my money. To keep my business, you must offer something better than they. **I am your customer now,** but you must prove to me again and again that I have made a wise choice in selecting your store, your products, and your services above all others."

(An Anonymous Customer)

"We are what we repeatedly do. Excellence, then, is not an act, but a habit." (Aristotle)

Customer Service in the High Desert

What is customer service and how important is it?

Printed with the permission of the author, Michael Stevens

I by no means consider myself an expert on customer service, but having been in the workforce since 1968, I believe I have acquired enough experience to write about this subject. As consumers, you and I have the right to demand and expect superior service.

What do we mean by customer service? There is no universally accepted definition. Even if a person is treated poorly—as long as he or she is *served*—in a technical sense, he or she has received *customer service*. Therefore, many companies can legitimately promote the fact that they are concerned about customer service.

Customer service is more than just whether a service was rendered. It is also **how** it was rendered, **when** rendered, and the **attitude** of the person giving the service. I went to a fast food restaurant and part of my order was a large orange juice. When it was delivered, most of the juice was frozen. I took the juice back and asked the clerk to please exchange it for some not frozen. She served me. But she made me wait, acted as if she didn't want to do it, and she had the most evil look on her face as she did so. Was that customer service? She may have thought so because I got what I wanted. I say no, because she was in no hurry to accommodate me, and acted as if I was troubling her. Not once did she smile, not once did she apologize.

I define customer service as treating customers with respect and dignity at all times, trying to determine the best and most equitable way of giving the customer what he or she is seeking, and trying to view the situation from the perspective of the customer. Customer service means being honest and fair, and giving the customer no less than 100 percent of staff's efforts. Is this too lofty a definition? I don't think so. Is it realistic? Absolutely. I realize from my own experience that there may be portions of the definition that may be difficult to perform at all times. For example, it may not be necessary to view the situation from the perspective of the customer. What would it prove? If I can't do something for a customer for whatever reason, what does it matter that I see their request from their perspective? It **does** matter, because it allows me to be empathetic, and therefore, more willing to do the other part of the definition, namely "to determine the best and most equitable way of giving the customer what he wants."

So perhaps you can begin to see just how complex this issue of customer service can be. It sometimes becomes a matter of perception.

It is quite possible that a person could be in top form, providing what he or she believes to be excellent service, only to discover that the recipient is dissatisfied or angry. How could this be? Somewhere along the line, "wires get crossed." If I walked into ABC Company, I should not have to communicate to their personnel that I expect to be treated fairly and with respect; that is what I call an "unspoken" expectation.

Whomever I may deal with at ABC Company should (hopefully) have the same unspoken expectation to treat me fairly and with respect, and expect it in return. As long as we both have the same expectation, chances are very good that the interaction will be positive. On the other hand, if I went into ABC Company and had unreasonable expectations—whether I communicated those expectations or not—the interaction is bound to be poor. What is unreasonable? For example, that I would expect the staff would drop what they were doing just to serve me, whether they were serving someone else or not. Unreasonable would be for me to expect that I would be provided special treatment, different from what other customers receive.

Here is a scenario that happened to me and I'd like for you to evaluate whether I had unreasonable expectations, if the company gave good customer service, and what would you have done as the customer or supplier?

The door handle on my minivan broke off. In order for me to replace it, I had to take apart the inside panel of the door. After disassembling the door panel, I discovered I didn't have the proper tool to install the handle. So, near the end of the business day (to not interfere with other appointments), I went to the local dealer from whom I purchased the minivan to ask if the service personnel would install the handle for me. They didn't have to remove the panel, and probably would take less than five minutes to use a certain tool (that I didn't have) to replace the handle. The dealer said to come back the next day, and the charge would be half ($27) of their hourly rate ($54). As a loyal customer, I didn't believe what I was asking deserved a charge. When I described to the service representative all that was needed, he didn't care. I asked for the service manager and he was less sympathetic than the service rep. At no point during the conversation did he say, "Let's take a look and see what we can do," or "Let's take a look and maybe we can show you how to do it." Instead, he debated with me and gave analogies regarding why he would not assist me. He didn't seem to want to work with me, or even care that I would leave a dissatisfied customer. He never made an effort to find a way to accommodate my request; all he was concerned about was his position.

How could this situation have been handled differently? Did I expect too much? What would you have done if you were the employer or if you were in my position, as the customer?

Note: I eventually purchased the tool to change the door handle; it was cheaper than having the dealer do it.

What you can do as customers or consumers to improve your chance of receiving good customer service: The strategies listed below are things you can do if you are not satisfied with the manner in which you were treated. For ease of understanding, the term *supplier* refers to the person(s) providing the service.

(1) Don't be intimidated. Many people don't like confrontations, believing that all confrontations are negative. Not true. Confrontations or encounters may be brought by negative circumstances, but the interaction doesn't have to be negative. If you patronize an establishment, you have the right to receive what you went there for (within reason, of course). It may be uncomfortable having to talk about your dissatisfaction with the manager or a person who may look frightening. Don't worry that there could be some retribution. If anything, you'll probably be treated better next time around because the supplier will know what you won't tolerate.

(2) Be assertive. If you don't stand up for your rights, who will? You are giving more power to the supplier if you accept shabby service, and in essence, are sending a message that says "It's OK to treat me as you do." If I were a manager or owner, I'd want to know how my employees were performing. You'd probably be doing the supplier a favor because they may not be aware that their behavior or performance is unacceptable. Your informing them will give them the opportunity to redeem themselves and correct the situation.

(3) Be clear, respectful, and communicate your expectations.
Don't expect the supplier to read your mind to know what happened, or to assume or interpret what you want to have happen. Don't ramble; just say

what you want or expect. Be respectful, and address the supplier by name or title, and avoid name-calling. Don't use profanity or resort to yelling or screaming. There's a saying that goes, "You catch more flies with honey than you can with vinegar."

(4) Try not to argue. If it appears that your first line of communication is getting you nowhere, don't argue. You may know you're right, but arguing tends to put people on the defensive and it becomes a struggle to see whose position will prevail.

(5) Seek the assistance from a supervisor or manager. Be respectful and first try to resolve the concerns at the lowest possible level. If, however, you have done this and are still dissatisfied, insist on seeing someone who has the authority to rectify the situation. Be prepared to accept the fact that a supervisor or manager may not be readily available and you may have to wait until later in the day or the next day.

(6) Put your concerns in writing. If, after trying the above-referenced strategies and you seem to get nowhere, continue to elevate your concern. Sometimes a concern is viewed differently by someone completely removed from the actual circumstance. If you resort to writing, be sure to describe circumstances in chronological order, careful to include names, dates, times, and results. Be sure to make a specific request regarding what you want to have happen. Leave a phone number where you can be reached and request a written reply to your letter.

(7) Be flexible and willing to compromise. There will no doubt be times where your request or your expectations simply cannot be honored. Compromising is not admitting defeat; it just creates a better circumstance for a win-win situation. There will be times, of course, when you may not want to, or when you should not compromise. You'll have to be the judge of the circumstances. Sometimes when you experience inferior service, it may only be an isolated circumstance brought on by who-knows-what. It may foretell or expose a serious problem that needs to be brought to light. Again, you'll have to judge and decide if you want to take responsibility for correcting a bad situation or simply walk away and leave it to someone else to deal with.

The root at each of these strategies is communication. The supplier of service cannot improve substandard service if he or she is unaware. Although these strategies seem to place the burden for correction with the customer, that is not completely the case; good customer service is a 50-50 proposition.

The strategies listed for what the supplier can do are both preventive and corrective.

(1) Create an environment and set clear expectations, which stresses provision of quality, superior, excellent customer service.
Management plays a key role in determining how employees will perform, especially employees who interact with the public (whether by phone or in person). Managers should have a written policy, display that policy, and practice the policy on a regular basis. Remember, though, customer service should also be kept in mind between employees.

(2) Seek and provide training.
Don't assume that employees are prepared to know how to interact with the public. If no one is qualified to provide customer-service training in house, send employees out, or hire a consultant to provide the training. Employees will feel more confident that not only do they know the company's policy, they also have the tools and knowledge to implement the policy.

(3) Empower staff.
Make staff feel like they're part of the process—and therefore the solution—by granting them the authority to make decisions to handle situations at the lowest possible level. As long as the company's expectations are clear and as long as training has been provided, suppliers should feel confident and competent to handle situations between customers.

(4) Appoint an ombudsman.
Suppliers who have the resources to appoint an ombudsman can significantly improve their chances of receiving public relations dividends. The ombudsman is a person to whom the public and employees can turn, to assist with problem resolution. This individual should be someone with superb people skills. The ombudsman should not be seen as someone to whom employees automatically or arbitrarily refer. The ombudsman should be a last resort if front-line personnel can't handle or resolve a situation.

(5) Know when and to whom to refer.
In the absence of an ombudsman, employees should know who should be contacted when a

situation is not easily resolved at the lowest level. Nothing is more frustrating and aggravating than to be told to see "so-and-so" or talk to "so-and-so," who in turn has to refer to "so-and-so" and on it goes up the management levels. Informing employees about who has what responsibility and authority to handle which situations that will minimize the frustration factor.

(6) Don't arbitrarily or immediately say no. Seek alternatives.

Nothing infuriates me more than to encounter a supplier who is so rigid that they would never entertain the idea of trying something different. When a customer makes a request that may be out of the ordinary or unusual, try to determine if the request has merit. Try to visualize the request from the customer's perspective. Even if the supplier seeks to explore alternative choices and has to come back to "no," he or she will be seen as trying to find the best and most equitable way of giving the customer what he or she seeks.

(7) Know how and when to compromise—and when to hold

firm. Some customers are unreasonable beyond belief, and have to understand that they will never get what they want. Some customers create problems for themselves either because of something they said or did, or didn't say or do. In either case, suppliers can't always be expected to acquiesce to customer demands. Even when a supplier must be firm, it's best to do so with kindness and respect.

(8) Don't be argumentative. If a customer has lost control and appears angry, circumstances will worsen if the supplier engages in argument or debate. Some strategies that might defuse the situation are:

- Use "sir" or "ma'am" when addressing the customer. It says, "No matter how you behave, I will treat you courteously and with respect, and I hope you will do the same."

- Get the angry customer away from the other customers. Angry customers tend to "grandstand," and try to show that they'll put the supplier in his or her place. Simply ask the person, "Would you please come with me and let's discuss what happened?"

- Make the customer comfortable; offer a beverage or somewhere to sit.

- Offer a consolation. Maybe the customer couldn't get what they wanted or weren't treated like they want to be treated; offer something that will make amends without making it appear as a bribe.

(9) Apologize. It's best to apologize, even if an allegation has been made and not confirmed. For example, if a customer complains about service received, the manager could say, "I'm sorry that you feel that way." It doesn't say that the employee was wrong or bad, but what it does say is that the manager is concerned about the customer's perception of the staff and establishment, and that their opinion is valued. It is definitely advisable to admit to and apologize for bona fide mistakes. To overlook the mistake or try to cover it up shows a "holier than thou" attitude, and makes it appear that the supplier is superior to the customer.

(10) Solicit ideas from customers and employees. The most effective way to get employee buy-in to provide quality customer service is to allow them to have ownership about what can be done. Employees are responsible for carrying out the policies, procedures, and values of the company. Their cooperation is obtained more easily when employee opinions are solicited. Don't solicit unless you are prepared to adopt and implement. This also holds true for customers. If you have a suggestion program, you'll be seen as a hypocrite if you only ask and not use some of the suggestions.

(11) Reward and command. Take time to acknowledge employees for their support of the quality customer service principles. Be sure to make the acknowledgements public, either at a staff meeting or an award program or employee newsletter.

(12) Share letters and calls with employees. Whenever letters or calls are received, let the employees know. The good letters and calls confirm that the employees are being successful in their efforts at providing good customer service, and the bad suggests that more work needs to be done. Acknowledge the employees who may have been referenced when sharing the good letters, and use only generic terms (an employee, an associate) when sharing the bad.

(13) Take disciplinary action for substandard performance.
The form of disciplinary action can run the gamut, but employees need to believe that management is serious about its commitment to provide quality customer service. Employees unwilling or unable to support management's commitment can either be trained, retrained, or dismissed.

(14) Use decoys. The best way to put to the test whether suppliers subscribe to the expectations of the company is to periodically test them. **Do not use decoys without letting employees know** that there is a possibility that they will be tested and tested randomly. There shouldn't have to be negative circumstances in order to try to determine how employees perform.

(15) Follow through. When suppliers make a commitment to do or not do something—especially if what was promised was designed to correct a customer concern—make sure there is follow-through. And follow through in a timely manner. Some changes will take longer than others, but communicate to the customer an approximate (and realistic) timeframe in which the commitment will be honored.

Who loses because of poor customer service? Everyone loses, the customer and supplier. The customer loses because he or she is left with a negative impression as the recipient of poor customer service. The supplier loses because they must now have to feel the possible effects of losing customers and developing a poor reputation.

Remember: Customer service is treating all customers with respect and dignity at all times, trying to determine the best and most equitable way of giving the customer what he or she is seeking, and trying to view the situation from the perspective of the customer. Customer service means being honest and fair, and giving the customer no less than 100 percent of the supplier's effort.

"Quality Customer Service. It's what we all should strive to provide, no ifs ands, or buts." (Michael Stevens)

So you want the day off. Let's take a look at what you are asking for.

- There are 365 days per year available for work.

- There are 52 weeks per year in which you already have two days off per week, leaving 261 days available for work.

- Since you spend 16 hours each day away from work, you have used up 170 days, leaving only 91 days available.

- You spend 30 minutes each day on coffee breaks. That accounts for 23 days each year, leaving only 68 days available.

- With a one-hour lunch period each day, you have already used up another 46 days, leaving only 22 days available for work.

- You normally spend 2 days per year on sick leave. This leaves you only 20 days available for work.

- We are off for 5 holidays per year, so your available working time is down to 15 days.

- We generously give you 14 days vacation per year, which leaves only one day available for work and I'll be darned if you're going to take that day off!

*** Frankie & Johnny Collectibles

Self Esteem

Appreciating my own

worth and **importance** and

having the **character** to be

accountable for

myself and to act

responsible for others!!!

Anonymous

INTEGRITY, SELF-RESPECT, AND SELF-ESTEEM

CHAPTER THREE

Are you a person of integrity or duplicity? If you say you are going to do something, do it. That shows integrity and builds character. Character is something we demonstrate regularly, not just once in a while. Do you behave the same in public as you do at home? People with integrity are the same wherever they are. People with integrity set examples for others. People often do what they see others do, especially children. People in leadership would be wise to model their integrity principles consistently.

> **"Integrity is doing the right thing, even when nobody is watching."**
> **(Jim Stovall)**

One thing I have noticed with our generations of students and young adults is that many of them don't return phone calls. When I ask applicants or students why they did not return my calls or correspondence, their reply is usually that they were busy or forgot. Some don't keep their scheduled appointments with me and don't call to reschedule. Many times after I have completed all their paperwork and have set up their jobs, they decide they don't want to go to work. Sometimes you can't even give people a job.

I have employers I have to call several times before they call me back. Sometimes they just don't get the messages. Many times that is due to their employees not writing the messages down and making sure they get to the right people. There are many who will tell you they are going to do something and then they never do it. We should not make promises we can't keep. People may doubt what you say, but they always believe what you do. Always strive to be excellent at everything you do. Work and act as if you were working for God! He sees everything you do. It has been said, "There is no traffic in the extra mile."

> **"A thousand words will not leave so deep an impression as one deed."**
> **(Henrik Ibsen)**

Something else I find interesting is that some days, it seems that people don't look in the mirror before they leave their homes. It is amazing how many people you see out shopping in curlers, their slippers, and in their pajamas. Also, there are so many young girls out in public with most of their chest hanging out. Are they striving for attention or asking for trouble? One day when I was at the post office, I saw an adult wearing his shirt inside out with the tag hanging out the back. I was almost compelled to say something when I changed my mind. He may have done it on purpose. Many teen girls are wearing short midriffs with their big bellies hanging out. Do they think that is attractive? Those must be some of the ones who have high self-esteem.

> **"I care not so much what I am to others as what I am to myself."**
> **(Michael de Montaigne)**

Self-esteem is how you feel about yourself and the value that you place on yourself. It is about your emotions and your feelings. It is something that you have to build on, just like anything else. Self-image is how we see ourselves. It is kind of like a portrait that we may carry around in our minds and hearts. The way we see ourselves is not always the way we are. You may want to ask others how they see you. We are always hardest on ourselves. Self-image is a concept of your identity and an understanding of your abilities. In the Bible, Genesis 1:26-27 says, "We are made in God's image."

Einstein and Edison were both told that they were poor students and dumb. When someone tells you that you can't, your internal response can tell you, "I can." Those who have low self-esteem or are depressed are that way for various reasons. Maybe they are not motivated to work or anything else. Some may have been victims of emotional, psychological, physical, and/or sexual abuse. If someone tells you that you are worthless, it can damage your self-esteem in a hurry. Fortunately, poor self-esteem is something you can repair. As Joyce Meyer once said, "You can be confident even when you don't feel confident."

One way to help repair self-esteem is by using affirmations. Affirmations are positive statements about yourself. If you have children, you want to make sure to give them affirmations. Our kids need as many positive strokes as they can get. Always find something positive to praise your kids for, even when they have misbehaved. Remember: They grow up and will often act the same way to others by the way they were treated. For example, if a child is constantly abused, he or she may take that abuse into his or her future family. Most of all, don't forget to hug your kids often and tell them you love them.

Affirmations can help you to have a more powerful and positive outlook on yourself and your life.

According to the King James Bible, "As a man think it, so is he and so does he become."

"One important key to success is self confidence. One important key to self confidence is preparation."
(Arthur Ashe)

WHICH ARE YOU NOW?

WHICH DO YOU WANT TO BE?

GOALS AND PERSEVERANCE
CHAPTER FOUR

"Think little goals and expect little achievements. Think big goals and win big success." (David Joseph Schwartz)

Many of the school personnel meet with students to find out what their plans are after high school. Many have set their goals and are on track for their futures. However, many don't know what they want to do and some don't even know if they want to work or where. That makes me question how long their parents are willing to keep them at home. Once kids are eighteen, we are no longer responsible for them, even though we still care and assist them whenever possible. I see too many twenty-two- and twenty-three-year-olds—who are perfectly capable of working and/or going to school—living with their parents or grandparents and doing nothing. It appears to me that some guardians are just not strict enough and are actually enabling them to do nothing. I have seen it firsthand with many young teens. I always told my son that once he turned eighteen and wanted or needed to live at home for any length of time, he would have to pay me $100 for rent and give me money for the car. He did just that until he moved out. How else are we going to teach our kids to become independent?

Some graduating students have dreams of becoming NBA players and have never been involved in sports, been on a team, or researched what it takes. Some want to be chefs, models, doctors, singers, and recording artists, and make plans to move. Yet they have not done any research. It is great and vital to have dreams, but we also need to plan to work toward those dreams.

There was once an old pilgrim who was making his way on foot to the Himalayan Mountains in the bitter cold of winter. As it began to storm, an innkeeper asked him, "How would you ever get there in this kind of weather?" The old man responded cheerfully, "My heart got there first, so it will be easy for the rest of me to follow." When have you thrown your heart into a dream, knowing that it was just a matter of time before the rest of you would show up?

My suggestion is as soon as you know what it is you want to do or be, take some classes, get on a sports team, join a club, get a job in that area, job shadow someone, and do research. The best way to find out about a job or career area in which you are interested is to talk to people who are doing that job or talk to those who hire. This method is known as informational interviewing. It is often a foot in the door and an extremely effective tool for finding a job and or deciding what you want to do or not want to do.

An informational interview is not applying for a job. It is strictly obtaining information about a specific job or career. I have enclosed a sample sheet on how to conduct an informational interview. Many people often obtain a job after doing this.

(See attachment in chapter twelve.)

Without goals or purpose, you have no direction. Sometimes when we don't plan, life gets in the way and we end up taking a detour. For example: A young graduate plans to become a nurse, but suddenly, she finds herself pregnant. Immediately her life takes a different turn. It is often difficult to get back on the original path. But all things are possible with discipline and determination.

> **"The road to success is almost always under construction."**
> **(Anonymous)**

A goal is a commitment to affect change. Fear or lack of time or direction often keeps people from achieving their goals. With goals, you want to dream or go as far as you can see. Because once you get there, you can always see further. Write your goals down, look at them often, and examine your priorities. You can put a picture board together of all the things you hope to accomplish. Try to imagine what you want and see yourself achieving it. Goals need to be attainable and measurable. A goal needs to be something you want, something you see yourself doing. It needs to be specific. It needs to say how much and by when. Always make short-term goals and long-term goals. You can live your dreams; your present situation does not have to determine where or how far you can go. Those who do not have goals are often taken advantage of by people who do.

We need to determine our passion and find out what stirs us up. Perhaps if you help enough people get what they want, maybe you will end up getting what you seek.

Zig Ziglar once made a similar statement.

"You have not failed until you stop trying." (Anonymous)

PERSEVERE! Never give up! Everyone has problems at some time in their lives; the only ones who don't are in heaven or that other place. It has been said, "Every problem has a solution, and every problem has a purpose." Consider changing your thinking by the way you respond to problems and pressures and stop rehearsing your problems. Sometimes we have to take life as it comes, one day at a time. It is important to keep your attitude positive, irrespective of whether things are going smoothly or not. Try to look at your problems as opportunities, which can be worked out for your own benefit. No matter how hard it is and how long it takes, victory is indeed possible. It is worth remembering that Thomas Edison failed 32,000 times before his light bulb became viable.

"Perseverance is falling nineteen times and succeeding the twentieth." (Julie Andrews)

> **"The ultimate measure of a man is not where he stands in moments of comfort and convenience, but where he stands at times of challenge and controversy."**
> **(Dr. Martin Luther King Jr. , Strength to Love, 1963)**

Consider the farmer and his donkey:

One day, a farmer's donkey fell down a well, and the donkey cried piteously for hours. The farmer said, "How am I going to get my donkey out?" He finally decided the animal was old and the well needed to be filled in, donkey and all. He had all his neighbors come over and he explained the situation. They all grabbed shovels and began shoveling dirt into the well. At first, the donkey realized what was happening and he cried horribly. (Sound like anyone you know?) "Everything is coming down on top of me!" After a while, the donkey became quiet. A few shovel loads later, the farmer looked down and was amazed at what he saw: The donkey was doing something amazing; he would shake the dirt off and step on top of it! As the farmer's neighbors continued to shovel dirt into the well and onto the donkey, the donkey would shake if off and step on top of the pile. Everyone was amazed when the donkey finally stepped over the edge of the well and trotted off!

The very dirt that tried to bury him ended up saving his life.

> **"Persistence and moral courage don't guar-antee victory, but they prevent defeat. In the game of life, we win something every time we overcome our fears."**
> **(Michael Josephson)**

MOTIVATION & AFFIRMATIONS

CHAPTER FIVE

"If you create an act, you create a habit. If you create a habit, you create character. If you create character, you create a destiny."
(Andre Maurois, French Author 1885-1987)

We all do what we want to do and what we don't want to do. Unmotivated people are that way because they choose not to be motivated. There are times when we may feel we are in a rut or everything is repetitive and we are just going through the motions. Sometimes we may feel empty inside, not knowing what our purpose is here on Earth. Sometimes people lose hope and turn to drugs, alcohol, compulsive buying, sex, pornography, or bury themselves in work to try and fill a void. However, none of those vices can fill the hole or emptiness you may feel. Each of us has a need for more. What we need to keep in mind is that no matter how bad things seem at times, there is always hope. Hope gives us confidence. We may need to refer to our Creator and depend on him. We are all created for a purpose in this life. I believe that this life is just a dress rehearsal for the next. That alone should be enough to motivate us.

Motivation is the key to getting going. But, how to get motivated is the question. Having a positive attitude is very important to being self-motivated. Someone once said, "Your attitude is your thought life turned inside out." Which means your attitude comes out of your mouth. Employers also look for the three A's—attitude, attitude, and attitude. You need to determine what motivates you, then go after it. Do not always go by your feelings. If you keep thinking about something in your mind, eventually your body will end up going there, whether it is positive or negative. Imagine those moments when you are craving something sweet to eat. Haven't we all been there?

Let us say you wake up one morning and you have a terrible headache. You get to work and the first person you encounter says, "Good morning, how are you?" You reply, "Oh, I have a headache." Later, you see someone else, they also ask how you are, and you tell them you have this horrible headache. All day long, you end up confessing to those you encounter that you have this horrible headache. Our words become our actions. The more you say you have a headache, the more you may be nurturing that headache. Why not try something positive instead? You could just tell yourself, "I am not impressed with this headache, and I refuse to accept it as such!" Take some aspirin. When you feel a cold coming on, why not repeat to yourself, "I am not getting sick, I am not getting sick." And often, you won't. Granted, there are times where you do get sick and have to take care of yourself. But for those times when we wake up not feeling right for no apparent reason, the more likely it will emerge that we won't go to work or school that day because of how we feel. We may not truly be sick that day; we may just be going by our feelings. It is within our power to change such thinking. It just takes a little practice.

When you wake up in the morning and have such feelings, have a conversation with yourself. Say positive things. "I can do all things I need to do." Fortunately, I do have another day. "Greater is he that is in me than he that is in the world." You may be surprised what you can motivate yourself to do. You should wake up each morning with a grateful heart and be enthusiastic. Remember: Some won't wake up the next day. So there is always something to be glad about. Do not be controlled by your feelings. More often than not, our battles are won (or lost) in our minds, and there are many external forces that come in to our consciousness to distract us. We need to recognize those thoughts and channel them to more positive territory. It's rather like changing the channels on your TV.

We have to learn to encourage ourselves. Listen to music, something inspirational or self- help tapes, or exercise, whatever it takes to get you going. Keep yourself motivated in order to motivate others. It's a daily challenge to be sure. We all have to motivate ourselves in order to motivate others. I keep motivational pictures in my office and at home. You can do whatever you set your mind to do. It just takes discipline.

> **" The most powerful thing we can do to change our lives is to change how we think."**
> **(William James)**

Affirmations are positive statements about you. They are short, specific, and goal-oriented. Affirmations start with "I am," "I have," or "I will." For example, "I will be living in a beach house by 2014." Begin saying what you are, what you want, and where you want to be as if it already is! "Call those things that be not as though they were." (Romans 4:17)

Start by making a list of positive statements about yourself, whether they are true or not.

When you look in the mirror every day, recite your positive declarations out loud. This can also be done in the shower, in the car, or periodically throughout your day. Then repeat your affirmations daily. It takes twenty-one to thirty days to make or break a habit. I highly encourage you to say positive things every day and see if your life and mood do not turn around.

Vince Lombardi said, **"Men decide their habits; their habits decide their future."**

For example, I am healthy, energetic, kind, giving, beautiful, wise, prosperous, and can do whatever I need to do. If you are in a slump or depressed, just say, "I am a very enthusiastic person who has many friends and a positive attitude." We can declare what we want and where we wish to be. By making a mental picture in our minds, we can focus on achieving our desired results. Try to orient your life to follow your expectations. We absorb what we constantly think about. Don't think or say another negative thought!

**"As you begin changing your thinking, start immediately to change your behavior. Begin to act the part of the person you would like to become. Take action on your behavior. Too many people want to feel then take action. This never works."
(John Maxwell)**

(See enclosed sample of affirmation list in chapter twelve.)

TIME MANAGEMENT & BALANCE

CHAPTER SIX

Time management has a great deal to do with work ethics! Time is such a precious commodity, yet many of us often take it for granted. Time management has less to do with managing your time than learning to manage yourself more effectively.

Thomas Edison once said, "There is time for everything."

It seems we live in a world controlled by numbers. There are clocks in our homes, schools, businesses, and cars. Most of us wear wristwatches. Virtually everything we do revolves around time and numbers.

What time is it?

When is dinner?

How old are you?

How much does it cost?

The speed limit is fifty-five, you work from eight to five, you play eighteen holes of golf.

Need information? We dial 411. Have an emergency? Call 911.

Holidays, taxes, and events all revolve around times and numbers. The list is endless.

To state the obvious, there are 7 days in a week, 168 hours in a week, usually 30 days in a month, 365 days in a year. It is the twenty-four hours in a day that are the key for us. To manage it efficiently, we need to determine our priorities each day or others will decide for us. Many times, we just need to learn to say NO! If we can learn to set our own priorities, then we can better achieve our goals.

Someone once said, "Don't prioritize your schedule, schedule your priorities."

We all have the same amount of time in a day. We just use it differently. Some are always in a hurry to get things done. Others are more relaxed and less concerned about time. Successful people are goal-oriented. Those who are truly productive are so because they set their priorities and schedule their time accordingly. All-too-common excuses include "I am too busy" or "I do not have time."

"Lost time is never found again."
(Ben Franklin)

If you want more information on time management, please read my book, *Self-Management to Time Management.*

"I have time for whatever I need to make time for."
(Robin L. Rask)

BALANCE

**"If you work, work, and when you play, play. Don't get the two mixed up."
(Jim Rhon)**

There is a song called "Live Like You're Dying." Many of us say, "I'll be happy when I have a house, get married, the bills are paid off, have kids, lose weight, have more money, when we get divorced, when the kids move out, etc." Be happy now and enjoy what you have. You don't know how long you have left. Do not live in regret. "Oh, I wish I would have spent more time with my kids and my wife. I wish I would have apologized and told them how much I loved them before they died." Learn to make peace with anyone you may have odds with. You will never regret that. Every day can be special if you live your day as if it were your last. Try to do something every day or each week to make someone's day. Even, if it is just a friendly smile, or a kind greeting, a compliment, a phone call, or sending them a card.

There are many of us who have excellent work ethics. There are also those who are workaholics and need more balance in their lives. Some of us are workaholics by choice, some have no choice due to their employment, and others have copious amounts of responsibility. As a single parent, I have had to work more than one job to pay the bills and live a decent lifestyle. I also have all the responsibilities, therefore, I feel like a workaholic. I do, however, make the time for what is important and what I need to do. I always have goals and many commitments. Once those are fulfilled, I can take my vacations and time for me. As many responsibilities as I have, I always make time to shop, get my hair and nails done, and visit with family and friends when I can. We all have different work ethics and different styles. We are all unique and we all have different agendas and purposes for our lives.

No matter how much we work, we all need to have some balance in our lives. We all struggle with it due to work and all the pressures of life. We have kids and all their activities, spouses and their needs, and any array of domestic and social activities. It is no wonder we have so much stress in our lives. Knowing what our limits are is very important; that is why it is so vital to learn to say NO! Life is a marathon, not a hundred-yard dash. You have to make time for what is important—family, kids, spouses, fun, relaxation, and regrouping. Our minds need to rest too. We all need good, balanced relationships and learn to use wisdom. If you want to have more wisdom, read the book of Proverbs in your Bible.

You may need to schedule your family events just as you might schedule appointments at work. Sometimes I just need to have time alone, including not answering the telephone. For me, in order to have time off to rest and regroup, I need to get out of town. A simple day at the beach with your kids and a book, watching and listening to the waves, and the other attractions can be very tantalizing. Changing the way we start out our day may alleviate stress and frustrations. No matter how busy we are or how many responsibilities we have, we need to prioritize the things that are important. We all must figure out what works best for us and do it. Below is a quote that hit home to me this year. In all you do, strive for balance and peace.

> **"Imagine life as a game in which you are juggling five balls in the air. You name them—work, family, health, friends, and spirit—and you're keeping all of these in the air. You will soon understand that work is a rubber ball. If you drop it, it will bounce back. But the other four balls—family, health, friends, and spirit—are made of glass. If you drop one of these, they will be irrevocably scuffed, marked, nicked, damaged, or even shattered. They will never be the same. You must understand that and strive for balance in you life."**
> **(Brian Dyson, CEO of Coca Cola Enterprises from 1959-1964)**

The Lost Dr. Seuss Poem

I Love My Job!

I love my job, I love the pay!

I love it more and more each day.

I love my boss, he is the best!

I love his boss and all the rest.

I love my office and its location. I hate to have to go on vacation.

I love my furniture, drab and grey, and piles of paper that grow each day!

I think my job is really swell, there's nothing else I love so well.

I love to work among my peers; I love their leers, and jeers, and sneers.

I love my computer and its software;

I hug it often though it won't care. I love each program and every file.

I'd love them more if they worked a while.

I'm happy to be here. I am. I am.

I'm the happiest slave of the firm, I am.

I love this work, I love these chores.

I love the meetings with deadly bores.

I love my job—I'll say it again—I even love those friendly men.

Those friendly men who've come today.

In clean white coats to take me away!

"On you will go, onward up many frightening creek, though your arms may get sore and your sneakers may leak."
(Dr. Seuss)

COMMUNITY OPINIONS ON WORK ETHICS TODAY!

CHAPTER SEVEN

Communities speak out!

"The people who make the most significant contributions are often not the smartest or the most skilled: They energize and encourage others." (Michael Josephson)

Dayna Yorba-Ruiz, Victor Valley High School WorkAbility and Liaison:

Coming from the other side of the fence in my prior job, most of my clientele with the county were already affected by all the issues you (Robin) discussed, which in turn, led to a large majority of them being jobless and on assistance. I think there is definitely a generational issue in the sense that parents without work ethics or skills are raising children without work ethics and skills.

When there is no foundation or example for success, I don't see how a child is fully able to grasp this if they don't see it happening at home. Although we are able to serve as positive role models for these students, and provide them with the skills and tools necessary for success, there are a lot of factors, which may contribute to their failure of lack of success. Even if we do help build up an awareness and enthusiasm for work, students may find that there are several factors working against them at home. One large factor is lack of support or actual discouragement to work from family. This could be due to cultural issues (many cultures still believe that a woman's place is not to be successful in education or the workforce, but to take care of the family at home instead). I also think that due to economics or demographics, many students are overwhelmed by excessive responsibility at home, therefore damaging work performance and reliability.

Many parents believe that a child's obligations to their family should come before work or school, even when it's things like babysitting other siblings. I also believe that other home issues affect a student's success at work, such as violence, emotional and financial instability of the parents, and moving around from house to house, family member, or foster home to foster home.

As far as adults, due to welfare reform, I think our programs are spending a large amount of money to put people to work, and pursue an education for people who just don't have the desire to do so. Many of these people go through life only desiring to meet the bare minimum requirements for everything to continue receiving all forms of aid. This may be a huge reason for problems in your R.O.P. classes. [ROP stands for Regional Occupational Program.] Some people are forced to either go to school or work, so they choose school as an option to continue receiving aid, and put forth little effort or drop out until they are discovered by their caseworker. Then they play the same system over and over again. With the type of people who are moving to the high desert, it will only keep getting worse since these lifestyles are following them here as well. The high desert is located about sixty-five miles northeast of Los Angeles, California. Please don't get me wrong: I have seen many success stories and I have felt excited and proud for the families I have been able to help.

Bridgette A. Browning, M.A., clinical director:

Let's consider today's youth and the four-letter word: **work**. *In my humble opinion, work is a core value taught in preschool years in the home. Simple chores like cleaning one's room, doing dishes, taking out the trash, cleaning the yard, feeding and walking the dog are elementary chores most high school [students] balk or rebel at doing when they have instant access to iPods, cell phones, TV, PCs and junk food! The old saying "idle time is the devil's workshop" applies. Many youth are screaming for rules, regulations, and boundaries of specific details how they can ease through any semblance of work so they have more free time to be LAZY! Every day I hear a youth say, "I am bored" or "There is nothing to do." Excuse me? Read a book, visit the nursing home, volunteer at the Red Cross or with Special Olympics, do your homework, obey your parents, attend your place of worship, etc!*

Youth are the future! They possess energy, enthusiasm, and excitement. They can make a contribution by getting involved in a purpose with passion to make a difference in our community. They can communicate, cooperate, and collaborate to build a coalition to stop gangs and achieve self-worth that they are involved in being a formidable answer to many of today's problems: alcohol and substance abuse, violence, sexual assault, anger management, low self-esteem, etc.

Renate I. Longoria, RNC, MSN, manager, education and infection control, Victor Valley Community Hospital, California:

> *I agree with you, Robin. Over the last twenty-five years, the work ethics really has changed. I was raised similar to you: strict, be responsible for your actions, and accept the consequences of any action that you did.*
>
> *Additionally:*
>
> *Be punctual to appointments; if you are late; apologize for any inconveniences you might have caused.*
> *Complete assignments/come to work on time, be positive and listen attentively.*
> *Be respectful always.*
> *Use appropriate dress code and language skills.*

Parental support is very necessary—not only should parents be there for their children; they also should show and demonstrate a behavior that their children should follow. Children watch their parents and follow their behavior.

I don't know if our values overall have changed or if it is our age! I remember in the '70s, when the hippie period evolved with the sexual revolution, etc., our parents—who were raised in the '20s and '30s—thought the world was coming to an end regarding our values.

Maybe we are having a "morals revolution." But I still think that there should be certain social expectations that should be taught to our youth who eventually will become parents themselves. Core values (i.e. treat with respect, being courteous, and self-respect) should be part of our upbringing no matter when we were born. I also think with the evolution of technology i.e. computers, iPods, Think Pads, and children getting more today than we ever did has somewhat a negative effect on our society.

Kathleen Oles, supervisor / Workforce Development Department, County of San Bernardino, California:

I believe much of what you say, Robin, has merit. I am of the firm opinion that part of the problem with the younger generation today is that they are not made accountable for their actions. Many parents today make excuses for their children's behavior rather than correct it. It is much easier to raise children by saying, "My child would never do anything like that," than to accept that all children are capable of doing just about anything. That it is our job as parents—to teach them, correct them, and accept that they will make mistakes and guide them through those mistakes. If you don't think they can do anything wrong, then you can just ignore the problem and hope it will go away. I also think that many parents nowadays are afraid to tell their children "No." They give in to their kids' demands because they don't think their kids should ever be unhappy. Guess what? You end up with spoiled, willful children who expect to get everything they demand. My daughter is a parent of two now and here are some of the difficulties she is experiencing:

The issue is kids getting everything they want. All her kids' friends have gigantic birthday parties every year either at Chuck E. Cheese's or at home with a bounce house, etc. Each kid's birthday is like Christmas, with tons of expensive presents. This is expected and parents act surprised if she says she does not plan to have a big party for her child's birthday. She has said to me: "It is difficult to parent nowadays because parents are under such scrutiny." If your child is screaming in the store, some people get mad if you don't do something about it—and others will report you if you do. I think it is difficult for people like her, who want to raise their children with proper discipline, manners, and the understanding that not everything in the world revolves around them. Does that make sense? I do think it affects their behavior later on when they go to work. They have not been reprimanded for bad behavior, they object to any criticism, and expect to have everything they want handed to them. There is a definite attitude that they should not be subjected to rules and regulations and are being mistreated if they are expected to conform.

Cynthia Lyles, parent, Georgia:

I have observed many of the same poor work ethics you have, Robin. I was having lunch at a Chili's restaurant in Duluth, Georgia about a week before Christmas. I ordered a bowl of soup, and water with lemon.

The server, who was a young college student at a local art school, brought my soup to me without a plate under the bowl. My spoon was stuck in the crackers. When I asked where my spoon was, he said, "There it is right there," pointing to the crackers. I then asked if I could please have a plate to place my soup bowl on. He said, "My bad," and he brought me another plate and soup spoon at my request. (Mind you, this was all done in his own good time.) I did not leave a tip.

Minimum wage here in Georgia is $5.10 an hour. There are help wanted signs everywhere. I believe the young people with a *good, mature work ethic are using their skills in more lucrative e-commerce jobs. For example, one young man who is a senior in high school makes 1,000-plus dollars selling products on eBay and teaching people how to create Web sites.*

I believe there are two groups of young people today: those who are self-motivated are using their home computers to make money. They are also starting their own small businesses, such as garage-door installation, car repair, handyman, painting services, and lawn services with parents or other family members, child-care providers, just to name a few. The other group are those who want something for nothing, slothful, lazy, with parents who buy them expensive name-brand shoes and clothing. They really think their parents' wealth is theirs and they are too good to work for minimum wage. If they do work for minimum wage, they are demotivated by the salary versus the job requirements. So they are basically hoping to get fired. It's not that they don't have the training or know-how. Most of them are just used to larger sums of money flowing through their hands.

Mary Lenz, high school work experience coordinator:

I agree with this totally. I had a student get a job and the employer told me he had a few situations where my student cussed him out. The student was not even aware this was a problem. So, I used this as an opportunity to teach my whole class, and was shocked to have them report even the managers cuss them out. I inquired what age these managers were and they were in their 20s. I have seen a big change in what is allowed on the job. Many of my students feel like, "Why work for minimum wage? I am worth more than that." They have no clue as to paying your dues and then working your way up.

Parent, employer, author, and business member of the community:

I have heard examples the past few years where High Desert employers have been frustrated by not being able to find qualified employees with good work ethics. If the problem is this bad, then that is frightening! Maybe we shouldn't have so much emphasis on providing classes in school that really won't determine whether a person succeeds in life or not and focus on "nitty-gritty" classes to prepare our young people for the real world. It seems that our school system is more concerned about students passing tests and achieving certain scores, but not equally concerned about student achievement and how they mature as a person.

Good for you, Robin, for bringing this to the forefront. It exposes some weaknesses "somewhere along the line," either in the homes of young people, schools, and perhaps even society for not demanding that we do a better job preparing our youth for adulthood. Perhaps it is a combination of all these things. Whatever the cause, we'd better figure out a way to reverse the trend or our country is going into further decline.

Student and teacher's aide at Victor Valley High School, California:

Kids today have too much freedom!

Syreeta Loudermilk, animal daycare manager, California

Lately, the students who have been doing their training with us have had the audacity to try and dictate when they will work, what hours they will be here, and some smart-mouth back. Some students start off OK and try, then toward the middle of their time here, they suddenly become lazy and feel they don't have to show up for work or call out. They seem to have a lack of respect for job ethics and for their elders. Some of the students have their parents call out sick, find out when they work next, tell me they are not coming on certain days.

I do think the training programs are beneficial but need a turning point. I think the students have too much control and input on these programs and it needs to be stricter for the students.

Leslie Poulsen, career technician (someone who provides resource information about choices after high school), California:

At what age do we become responsible for ourselves? When does that mental magic happen? How and why? When I first started thinking about this project, my focus agenda was addressing how other people should hold each of us accountable for our own actions. But that philosophy did not measure up for me. I want to be held responsible for my own determination of right and/or wrong.

My final observation concluded: What happened to each of us being responsible to ourselves for the principle of "right" conduct? The answer to this, I believe, is when the line of what is "right and ethical" behavior has become so faded and moveable that it now is allowed to suit a given situation to please ourselves. In the study of human behavior, how does one person just "know" ethical behavior and another have no perception of the meaning?

At this point, I am trying to discern if ethics are intrinsic or extrinsic. Maybe there is no true answer for all people. There are as many equations as there are human beings that would go into the finite conclusion that it is indiscernible.

Dan Weaver, manager, Gottschalks Department Store:

What I have seen and experienced in the last few years. I am sure that shrinks and analysts can give you all sorts of reasons that the young workforce does not have the work ethics of yesteryear, but from my own experience, I'd have to say it's more on an individual basis and not a blanket coverage of all. There seems to be more "kids" these days who don't have that work ethic but it is due mainly to what sort of background they are coming from. This generation is not a "teamwork" generation. Everything is individualistic so there is no importance placed by them on doing their best so that everyone succeeds.

They do everything by themselves, and the Internet is a perfect example. Everything they need to find or want is readily available to them with a stroke of a key. There is not a lot of hard work to get it. As such, they take that same attitude to work and it should be a lot of hard work to get what they want. Also, if it is repetitive, it becomes boring to them rather quickly. It's become a self-gratification generation and businesses have to learn to adapt to that; moving people around quickly from one area to another and giving them more and more challenges. This is hard for businesses to do in the entry-level, minimum-wage positions, thus, the huge turnover.

Also, kids these days are given more by their parents, and as such, expect more to be given to them from their employers, too. Most parents want their kids to have more than they had. Let's face it, our parents were the same. We had more then they had (especially if they came from the Depression era) and we have given our kids more too. They now expect more to be given to them even in the workplace. This again is not a blanket overall statement, as there are parents who have instilled a work ethic and it shows, but it is a growing trend that many have not, for whatever reason, and I leave that to the shrinks to figure out. What I have to do is adapt to the changing environment and offer the challenges they require to stay motivated at work. As in my case, 90 percent of the young kids starting out are not here for a career, but for a job to pay for gas, books, movies, etc., and as such will always be walking in and out the revolving door. But, while I have them, I need to get the most out of them by making the job, first and foremost fun, then challenging.

Josh, custodian and R.O.P. instructor, Victorville, California:

I have noticed that kids this year are the least productive students I have ever had. I even went the extra mile for them and provided them with the supplies they needed for their work portfolios. Their finished product was inferior to anything I had ever seen. I think our kids are disillusioned about life in general. Many of them display a cynical and disparaging form of motivation. I am not really sure where all this lack of enthusiasm and sluggishness comes from, or how to cure it. But, I am afraid that the infection might get worse. It is as if though they are living in the lyrics of a song, "Money for nothing, chicks for free" by Dire Straits. It is possible that they are watching too much MTV, which is wearing away the image of what success really is. Subliminal advertising, as we know, can be used as a powerful brainwashing tool.

What can we do individually to counter this lack of motivation?

Manuael Diaz, personnel technician, Santa Cruz, California:

This is not an easy topic to put a rope around. It is like Jell-O: If you have a container, it will fit the shape that it is in, but try to scoop some up with your hand and it gushes through your fingers. If you are in a situation that reflects the conditions of work, you can then use those conditions to experience work. If you are a teacher, your classroom is a shop floor and you are the foreperson. Your workers are students and production is education. How do you get young people to apply themselves to education? Among the myriad of motivators, there has to be expectations placed on "workers." If you expect or tolerate low standards and motivation, that is what you will experience. Therefore, the applications of expectations in the form of discipline and pride have some effect, even when students react to it. Learning that there is work that has to be done is better than learning that work never has to get done.

The broader issue is that even we, as adults, have weak work ethics. What is the cause? Are we also a lost generation?

My view is that we, as workers and producers, are alienated from our labor. Our relationship to our work is as wage slaves. We have little control over what we produce, who can buy it, and the use that it is put to. It is no wonder that in a world that treats us second to products and cares little about our worth as people, we have little interest in giving up our life energies eight hours a day. Young people become so alienated that even in their free time, when no one is bossing them around, they do little that is productive and sometimes too much that is destructive.

If you are a teacher, boss your students around. It may be one of the few times in their lives that they are working at something worthwhile that someone is expecting them to do their best at and feel productive doing it. Better to be remembered as a pusher than as a pushover.

Mary Richards, LPN, Minneapolis, Minnesota:

One thing I know for sure is that people in general need to be taught how to work as a team. Working as part of a team does not mean working by yourself without any co-workers. Working with co-workers and supervisors can, however, be a challenge. People come with so many different personalities and points of view. Knowing how to take responsibility for one's own actions is another aspect a person needs to learn. Maybe there needs to be more community classes available to both young people and adults, to teach them how to be a part of a work environment. People need to learn how to work together to complete a project, not every person for him- or herself.

Roberta Fox, parent, job coach, and assistant facilitator, high school:

Worth ethics, I believe, are developed in the home. I also believe that work ethics have a great deal to do with common sense.

Many people who are shy should try and seek employment where they are basically secluded. Those who work with the public need an outgoing personality. I personally feel that companies try to "skimp" by hiring anyone and everyone. Many of the younger employees I have encountered, with ages ranging from sixteen to twenty-five, have a lot to learn. They are too busy on their cell phones, talking with fellow associates, and having friends visit. Many businesses employ younger managers who may lack some work ethics themselves or just do not know how to manage their employees. I feel that employers need to have ongoing training for managers that will help the younger workforce; the goal would be to have better employees with more motivation and desire.

Young employees seem pretty lax. They act like it is a chore to go to work every morning or every afternoon or every evening. Our young generation is too "pampered." My encounter with the younger generation of employees is really not good. My personal calculation receiving good service would be 10 to 15 percent. Let's take a "courtesy clerk" at a grocery store, for example: "Would you like paper or plastic?" Well if I had to say that every day, maybe my attitude wouldn't be the best. But, what I have learned over the years—and the way I was raised—is that we have to make the best out of it. Look at "Would you

*like paper or plastic?" as a stepping stone. If, when going to
school, they are encouraged to know "this too shall pass," then
maybe their attitudes will be better. I feel at home is where they
lack the support. In today's society, there are so many divorced,
blended, and single-parent families. Taking all of these elements
into account, work ethics should be taught at schools, even at a
community college level.*

Job developer, Spokane, Washington:

*As a parent of six grown children and a prior job developer,
I see that employers do not seem to have protocol in place that
they use for excessive absences or poor work habits. Employees
call in sick whenever they want, and the employer has resources
in place to call in someone to take their place. It seems to be of
no concern to many employers. I wonder if this has to do with
part-time employment and no concern for overtime pay, as there
isn't any with part-time employees?*

Jeanne M. Johnson, Crescent City, California:

*This is a very serious problem in today's world; so many younger
adults just do not care. Some are just not interested in working,
even with good-income jobs. Instead, they are rude, talk back to
clients, walk out, or just do not show up for work at all—nor do
they call. "Why is this happening?" I look at what I have done
in my past and what I can offer, then ask myself when will this
all come full circle. Is it the parents? Is this the way children
are being taught? Are they being told or introduced to "please,"
"thank you," "excuse me," or "pardon me"? I am absolutely
positive with the answer: "No!" I was raised with respect for
my elders, and I followed the golden rule: "Do unto others as
you wish to be treated." Also, sometimes children are very mean
and hurtful; are they taught or shown this? Sadly not, it seems
to not be discussed and goes unnoticed in today's world. I wish
there was a magic wand that could be waved and all could see
what is really going on in today's society. With computers now,
so many are getting away with more bad behavior in cyberspace.
Adults are just now finding out what is really going on behind
closed doors.*

Could it be that we are not providing our young adults with more counseling as to what they want to be when they grow up, or really talking to them as a person and showing or sharing with them the real facts of life?

Jane Faytol, retail manager of a department store:

I have been in the retail field for over fifteen years and have participated in several educational programs for the past six years. There has been a significant change in the students currently in the programs compared to those six years ago. I believe that there are several factors that contribute to the decline in work ethics in the students. The moral ethics have declined as well. Here are several factors that I believe contribute to this issue. The factors are somewhat different between the R.O.P. students versus the WorkAbility/TPP and other programs. WorkAbility and TPP are funded programs that put students to work.

R.O.P. STUDENTS (Regional Occupational Program)

Most of the previous students have been bright, outgoing students who have come from two-parent homes. The only incentives are the credits given and the experience earned at the job site. The students are not generally motivated enough by these two factors alone, and the parents, from my experience, do not hold them accountable for their jobs sites. The students are usually in other extracurricular activities. There is a lack of time management given to school, worksite, and activities. Although both parents are present, both are usually working and some commuting to their jobs.

These students are being taught time management in class, but it appears that overall, it is not reinforced at home. The parents seem to lack control or knowledge of what their children are involved in after school. The general mentality is more "I deserve this job, I don't have to earn it." There is also an overall disrespect for elders and authority figures with this generation of students. I believe that this is also reinforced at home. I believe that the issues are more socially related than financially.

PAID TRAINING PROGRAMS

I believe that the issues and concerns are related more to the financial status of the families. The students often times come from low-income families, single parent, or have multiple siblings. There is a need for these students to contribute financially to the family income. The students' test scores are usually on the lower spectrum. I believe that the lack of proper nutrition, due to the family's situation, plays a role in the student's ability to focus and perform in school.

There were many incidents when the students only had one meal throughout the day, due to the lack of money, not the lack of time. This again affected their performance at the work site. The social aspect of this is that they are not socially as accepted by their peers because of their style of dress, the stigma of being in non-mainstream classes, and the inability to participate in extracurricular activities due to family responsibilities. In general, these students lack confidence. The opportunity is in their overall communication skill with each other and with adults.

Other factors that I believe influence the behavior of our students is media—audio and visual. The images are that of degradation of females and violence toward males. The rap genre has become mainstream, and the lyrics are negative and promote disrespect. The alternative genre portrays depression with angst-hidden lyrics. The music of today is not inspirational, nor does it promote knowledge. MTV is filled with reality shows that are creatively edited to fit their marketing purposes. The shows encourage teens to be materialistic. It, in general, defines a person by their possessions rather than their personalities. There are no longer shows that families can watch together that reinforce morals and ethics. Shows like Viva la Bam *indirectly encourage kids to disrespect their parents by verbal and physical abuse without any consequences.*

LACK OF AFTER-SCHOOL PROGRAMS SPECIFIC TO THE HIGH DESERT

The population has grown considerably; unfortunately the activities available to the students have not.

The existing community centers are not accessible to everyone, especially if they are not within walking/driving distance. The bus system does not reach out far enough. Even if the students are financially able, they must figure out how they will get to their activity.

Most parents have to work; this leaves the students unsupervised for the majority of the day. A large number of residents are relocating from the Los Angeles basin, which brings a different mentality. Young adults tend to get easily bored, and in turn, get involved with negative influences.

INCREASE IN HOME STUDIES

More parents are choosing to home school their children then ever before. Often times, the parent is not present during the day with their child. The child then gets involved in negative activities. The skills of time management and social interaction sometimes suffer due to a less-structured education.

GRANDPARENTS RAISING CHILDREN

The absence of the parents causes the grandparents to take over the responsibility. The generation gap is too much at times. The lack of understanding on the child's part becomes projected into disobedience. The grandparents are, at times, mentally and physically unable to discipline the children. This contributes to the cycle of teen pregnancy, and young parents who lack experience and knowledge to teach ethics. It seems never-ending.

These are obviously a few factors. There's so much more to be discussed. The educators need active participation from the parent(s) in order to see consistent progress. One organization cannot accomplish this alone.

Nettie Stocz, high school graduate and real estate office assistant:

What I have seen in the workplace for work ethics today frustrates me to no end. I have seen other employees come to work and they don't care about working. They are so busy talking on their cell phones to friends that their work doesn't get done, making my job ten times harder than what it should be. I am lucky if I get my job done. When I explain something to an employee on how to use the fax machine or how to make copies, they are too busy thinking about how to win a video game or what nail polish to wear the next day, instead of listening. When I ask them if they understand, they say yes when they have no clue what to do. When I go back and the job is not done, I ask if they understood what I told them. They then tell me they were not listening. Of course, there are those who do their work and are very productive. In conclusion, regarding work ethics, I believe that some just don't have any and some kids and adults just do not want to work, period.

Rochelle Powell, retail store manager:

Work ethics have gone so far downhill. First of all, the person looking for a job does not know how to come in to apply. Applicants come in with their kids, their families, and their mates. They do not know how to dress to come in and ask for a job application. If by some chance they are hired, they come in late and they want to tell you what they feel like doing. Or they just do not show up at all, or even make a phone call. They get upset when you cut their hours. Half the time, they do not want to perform the task they are given. If they do perform, nine times out of ten, it is not correct. We have even had some go to the back of the store and talk on their cell phones. Rules seem not to apply to them. They have their own mindset. When it comes to customer service, they feel they do not have to provide that. I could go on about this subject for hours.

Debra Foust, retail chain personnel manager

As a human resource director, I have noticed a steady decline in the quality of young people who apply for employment. When they come in for an interview, some act as if they are doing us a favor by applying for a job here. Some are unable to express themselves verbally. They do not dress to impress, and they lack the basic social manners that my generation was taught. The following are some things I have experienced while attempting to conduct an interview: gum chewing, cell phone ringing, wearing all facial piercing, inappropriate attire, strange hair color, poor manners, and lack of basic social skills. Our turnover is high because some young people feel jobs are easy to find. Once we hire them, we start having problems such as them coming in late, poor language, poor attitude, and just calling off for no real reason. Most young people today have no idea how hard it is to make a living today. They live for today with no plan for the future.

"We make a living by what we get. We make a life by what we give."
(Winston Churchill)

Katherine M. Munoz, employment and career workforce specialist:

Today's young adults lack work ethics: Several studies suggest the break-up of the family may be linked to why today's young adults lack work ethics. Many businesses and industry leaders agree that essential work ethics are key to getting hired and maintaining a permanent job. In fact, work ethics should be taught and practiced in order to develop an effective workforce.

In today's society, in many cases, both parents must work in order to financially support the family. Whereby, after school, many high school young adults are coming to an empty home or are having to raise themselves or take care of younger sisters or brothers. Without the parent's supervision or support, these young adults lack work ethics traits such as character, communication, appearance, organizational skills, cooperation, respect, a positive attitude, teamwork, and have a problem with attendance.

In order to correct this problem, parents need to be willing to spend more proactive time with their son or daughter. This would include the parents reorganizing the evening schedule. Every child is different, so the maturity and personality of each young adult should be an important consideration. Each parent should also think about assessing his/her young adult's needs and explore the various options available to them and remember that they are still in charge. Communicate with your son or daughter to establish codes of conduct and to teach responsibility and self-discipline. All parents must take their responsibility of their children seriously and consider their children's needs as they meet their work obligations. Whether physically present or not, parents must remain in charge.

This was part of an article published in a school newspaper in February of 2006

It has often been said, "That to succeed in high school it is necessary to have drive and ambition." However, many students seem to lack the motivation to be disciplined in school. One senior stated that in one of his classes, they do not do anything and time is foolishly wasted. Some students occupy their time by talking, playing cards, and listening to music. In many freshman classes, students are given little work to do and are often left on their own to complete their assignments. It seemed that those high school newcomers do not take advantage of the time they are given and would rather waste their time. This behavior continues despite the teachers' reminders that time is precious.

The lesson that "Learning is Imperative" appears lost on many of these young students. One of the causes appears to be apparent laziness and apathy on the part of the students.

Many students complain that the numerous classes, even school is just a waste of time.

Not all classes and students feel their time is wasted. Many students use their time wisely and get their work completed so they do not have to stress about it later. One senior states, "School is important to my future, so I try not to mess around too much. If you stay focused, it's not that bad."

Parent and daycare director:

Society has made it hard for us as parents.

Cathi Vargas, teacher's assistant, parent, and job coach:

> *I have been working with students for the last ten years. I have had the opportunity to work with a wide variety of students with disabilities. In my opinion, some students are more challenging than others. I also have had challenges with parents.*
>
> *The parenting skills of a student with disabilities requires more patience and discipline. Some parents do not seem to have the tools or knowledge to follow through. Therefore, the children are affected. It would be nice if everything for a disabled child were not such a challenge. But, we have to focus on what we can do to help those in need without such frustration.*

Travis N. Trestler, Indiana

> *This book project is personally fascinating to me because of the recruiting position I was in before publishing books. I'm twenty-seven, and see my peers every day, lacking the work ethic that was instilled in me at a young age. I wonder how we are going to stay on top of the economic world!*

From a visually impaired person's perspective:
John Gratz, child care worker, ages 12-22 for Lodge Makers, transitional president, board member, and former student:

> *Where have work ethics gone? In today's work world, I constantly come in contact with people who are thinking about what they can get for nothing, instead of what they can earn for a job well done. People seem to spend all their time making excuses for why they can't work or trying to put the blame on other people for why they are not doing a good job. You don't see many people anymore with self-respect who take responsibility for their own actions. People need to place value in a job well done without regard to what others say or do. The main thing I see lacking in the workplace is the desire of employees to show up on time and work their schedule—simply because it is the right thing to do.*

There is a belief that whatever you can get away with is the right thing to do. Employees in today's work world have a goal to do as little as possible and get paid as much as possible. I believe we need to get back to three basic work ethics: work hard for a living, you get out what you put in, and self-respect cannot be handed to you, it has to be earned. Work ethics are what you do when no one is looking.

From a counselor, employer, probation officer, and parent's point of view:

My thoughts on work ethic: I've experienced the whole range from excellent, over-the top-commitment to apathy.

I think it has much to do with parenting. Many of us do not allow our children to experience the natural consequences of their actions. I think the problem is partially rooted in co-dependent behavior. When we don't believe our kids can handle their consequences or don't believe in their ability to do certain things, we communicate to them that they are incapable. When we are acting in a co-dependent manner, we need our children to think well of us, and we act so their opinion of us is positive, often meaning we go easy on them and protect them from the consequences of their behavior/actions.

Our best teaching is by example. My dad always believed in doing his best, doing more, and giving more, and he rose to the position of vice president with a large retail chain. I learned some of his ethic. But for some reason, I was unwilling to work as hard as he did. My kids seem to have good work ethics. I think my example and their grandfather's example played a part, though I am guilty of over-protecting to some degree.

I guess in reflecting on the hundreds of kids I've hired, trained, and supervised, as well as worked with in school, I'd say the work ethic is learned behavior; if not from parents, perhaps a significant adult such as you, or me, or a family member, or a teacher, etc.

Employer Feedback & Worker Rights

Chapter Eight

Several students and adults have lost their jobs because they did not show up for work or call in to notify the employer. How hard can that be?

Others have lost their jobs because they had friends come in and spend too much time visiting, or their friends stole merchandise.

Some of the reasons applicants have lost their jobs before they started are:

- Not being able to fill out a job application, including the ones online.

- Not dressing appropriately when applying for a job or interview. Some ask for applications while shopping or dining.

- Some come in pairs or groups to apply; some bring their kids with them.

- Others simply don't show up for the interview.

Some other reasons students and adults have lost their jobs due to poor work ethics are:

- Not coming back from break or lunch.

- Excessive lateness and not being dependable.

- Stealing and lack of respect.

- Sexual harassment.

- Not calling in when they will be late or absent.

- Poor customer service.

- Standing around and not showing initiative.

- Talking back to the employer and being rude.

- Not following instructions.

- Poor dress code or not following the dress code.

- Poor attitude or poor listening skills.

- No enthusiasm for the job or smiling.

- Not motivated.

- Can't read, write, or count.

- Can't read a tape measure.

- Not being a team player.

- Not being honest.

- Not taking care of company tools or equipment.

- Not following safety rules or procedures.

- Just not showing up or quitting.

- Lack of social skills.

- Not having a social security number.

- Using their cell phones (this includes to check the time).

"Life is short, Focus from this day forward on making a difference."
(Winston Churchill)

James G. Cole / Charter Media Creative Services Manager

The **important** *characteristics I look for in an individual for hire are as follows:*

Integrity: *Be honest. When things don't go well on the job, and we all have bad days, don't make excuses or try to cover up mistakes. Learn from the experience, express concern, and relate what should have been done.*

Attitude: *Without a positive attitude on the job, training is next to impossible. One must be willing to learn, take notes when being trained and be willing to work hard while maintaining a positive attitude. Accept new challenges eagerly and follow through with a given task in a timely manner.*

Attendance: *Being punctual is also being reliable. An employer must be confident that an employee will be on time, whether it be for work, a client meeting or to open or close the business. It is inconsiderate when others count on you and you're late, which will often create a compromising situation for those relying on your presence.*

Appearance: *Having a neat and clean appearance is important. Clean attire, groomed hair, and appropriate jewelry are monitored by many professional organizations, therefore it is important to look neat and clean.*

Productivity: *When given a task, it is important your manager knows it will get done as directed and will be done on time.*

Organizational Skills: *Being organized on the job makes a great impression, it will usually make your work less stressful, at the same time making the workload easier to handle. Be observant and make constructive suggestions when you think there may be a better way to complete a task. Your ideas may not always get implemented, but over time, you may find it puts you in favor with management.*

Communication: *If you want to advance with the organization you're working for, effective communication is essential. You will enhance your value to your employer by keeping your manager informed about the progress of tasks. By keeping those in your organization informed, you save the firm time, money, and you will earn the respect from your manager, giving yourself an advantage when promotion is considered.*

Teamwork: *Working well with others is important to the workplace structure. Most jobs require individuals to work together to accomplish common goals for the good of the company. If you cannot work well with others to project deadlines, the job quality could be compromised. This is a disadvantage for everyone on a team. Cooperation is key for the success of any team, and as a result it will benefit the individual.*

In the fall of 2006, I attended an educators forum at a nearby hotel, with a panel of businesses. The employers all stated that there is a shortage of qualified applicants for their open positions and that it was mainly due to the lack of work ethics and basic skills. Those of us in attendance already knew they were preaching to the choir. Teachers, school personnel, parents, and students needed to hear this message. One employer said, "Applicants need to be able to read, do basic math, be able to fill out an application, know how to type memos, address envelopes, and have a strong work ethic."

The employers stated that the fastest growth is in transportation, warehousing, and utilities, and the logistic industry could bring lots of jobs. But who will fill these jobs was the question. The employers also stated that in some companies, there is a shortage of welders, electricians, dispatchers, and mechanics. There is also a big demand in inventory control. One of the trucking companies told us that some of the high-school graduates are making $75,000 to $100,000 a year, and UPS has a shortage of drivers. One of the employers representing a major airport said there were 6,000 jobs available.

Another employer stated what many applicants are failing to realize is that this is the technology age, and truck drivers and warehouse personnel need computer experience. So make your children computer smart and proficient. One audience member suggested having a training school within an organization so there would be more trained and qualified employees.

There seems to be a lack of knowledge and understanding in today's culture/generation on what it means to have a job and be a worker.

The good news is there are many who have and are acknowledging this serious situation. So in some areas, educators, students, and business leaders are working with the local workforce to turn things around. It will take **"all of us"** to make a difference and change our society to educate our future leaders of tomorrow.

In the fall of 2006, there was a comment in a newsletter that stated that the Inland Empire in San Bernardino, California had a company with 240 job openings paying $12.50 per hour that they cannot fill.

There is also a shortage of apprentices. There was an ad in one of the papers stating that by 2014, there will be a demand for more than 734,000 electrical workers. The president of IBEW, the Brotherhood of Electrical Workers, said the task ahead is not to just recruit and train more electricians but to make provisions to replace those who will retire.

The shortage is not only in America; there are an estimated 37,000 job openings in the UK. So there are plenty of job opportunities for those who want to work. Check with your vocational schools such as R.O.P. or community colleges, and union-sponsored apprenticeship. I have facilitated two major apprenticeship forums in the high desert of California, and there are plentiful jobs!

There is also a shortage of nurses, police officers, and firefighters. There was an article in a newspaper that said, "Anaheim, California is SHORT HANDED."

That means they need workers, including high school and college students. Try working for Uncle Sam! There are plenty of federal government jobs available.

Other Examples of Poor Work Ethics From Employers and Teachers:

As President Harry S. Truman once noted, **"It's not so hard to know the right thing to do; the problem is doing it."**

Some businesses can't hire good people because they cannot pass a drug test.

One of the grocery stores continuously hires because of various reasons with new applicants and employees.

One employer was calling an applicant for a job interview based on his résumé. However, when the employer heard the loud and offensive voice mail, he hung up without leaving a message. This is a reminder that first and second impressions do count, even on the phone.

A retail store in a mall had a student go on a break and not come back to work because she had an emergency with her mom. She never informed the employer. She did not get hired after her training.

A video store had a student from a training program who told the employer he did that job yesterday, so he felt like he did not have to do it again the next day, even though that was his job. He was let go, due to his poor attitude.

One department store had a student trainee from a program walk around and try on clothes and test out various perfumes. Later, that student did become successful somewhere else. They also had a student sit back in a chair one day with her feet up. Had the manager not seen her, she would have been hired. This same employer had a student tell an associate how to cheat the company. He was immediately terminated.

A heating and air-conditioning employer had a training student who could have cost the employer a major lawsuit because he did things that he was not supposed to do. (This could have been an awesome job.)

One home and gardening store had a graduate quit after the first two hours he was there. Why? Because he had to sweep and water plants on his first day as his first task, and he thought that was beneath him.

One business had a student who went to work and claimed he was there all day when he actually clocked in and went out another door. Mom picked him up at the end of his shift. Little did he realize that the company had him on videotape.

One teacher had a student she interviewed in class in preparation for the real interview, and her pupil did not do well. The teacher told the student what she needed to improve on, and that she still had two more weeks to prepare. When the student went on the job site interview, she did not get the job because she was not prepared, did not make eye contact, and was too scared. The employer stated that they needed a more outgoing personality for that job. The teacher then set up another job site for the student and explained to the employer that this student was very nervous and may not be as well-prepared as others. However, the student had a good personality and was responsible. The employers said, "No problem, we will have plenty for her to do so she will not be interacting with customers until she is ready." The teacher explained all this to the student. The student responded that she did not want to go through another interview and fail. She also told the teacher she was dropping the class. This was very heartbreaking for the teacher, since her student was nineteen, out of school, and had only six more night classes to complete the course.

I, Robin Rask, had a senior who needed six points to graduate. I told him he needed to fax a letter of recommendation to me within two days so I could pass him. He chose not to. I had one student who needed twenty-five points to pass the class to graduate. All he had to do was make out a thank-you card to the employer. How simple that was! But he chose not to. He did receive a perfect-attendance certificate and was very proud of that. We have seniors who are not concerned about graduating until the last minute. Then it is almost always too late. The bar was raised for a short period where a few schools no longer gave out D's or F's. The grading scale became A, B, C, and NP, indicating "non-proficient." If they did not pass with a C-, they failed. It saddened my heart because some of them really tried and did not deserve to fail. In the summer of 2007, the school board returned to the original grading process.

I also had a student who quit her job two weeks before the end of the semester because she thought she was failing. Somehow it never occurred to her to pick up the phone to discuss this with me or call the employer to let them know she was quitting. The frustration for me was that she was originally passing the class. However, because she quit, she did not get a certificate or her full units. This really boggles the mind. Of course we do have many students with great work habits and who do go the extra mile and become successful. "Congratulations to all of you!" I am very impressed when I see my students get hired and later see them working two part-time jobs!

There was one applicant who interviewed at a huge retail chain. During his interview, he was asked to fill out a job application. While he was filling out the application in front of the employer, he used his cell phone to call home and ask his parents questions. This was an immediate turn-off to the employer, and he was not hired.

I placed a high school student in the mall at a retail store for her training phase. She told the employer she could not work Sundays and could not work past 4:00 PM on Saturdays because she had to be in bed by 8:00 PM. I told the student not to plan on being hired, and she was not.

I also had two adults who were in their mid-twenties, whom I had placed into really good jobs. One was with a school district, and the other with a cable company. Just before it was time to start work, they quit the class, had their phone disconnected, and did not tell me. I wrote them each a letter and the letters came back.

A major employment agency had a man come in looking for work. The representative stated that he looked like he just crawled out of bed, hair uncombed, unshaven, and his clothes were wrinkled. When asked to provide his right-to-work documents, he only had his driver's license. He stated that his mother had his social security card, and he would have to go home to get it. He was told that if he was serious about looking for work and wanted the representative's assistance, he could return with his proper documentation. (This man was in his mid-forties.)

Another gentleman called employers, seeking employment as a Class-A truck driver. His sales pitch started out very positive and eager. Throughout the conversation, he commented on how he only had four points on his driving record: one accident and one D.U.I. He was upset that employers were not calling him back.

Another gentleman called employers, seeking employment in warehousing. He was selling himself over the phone with his experience and skills. As the employer asked more questions about the reason he was not working, the man was getting more desperate. He stated to the employer that he really needed to work and was willing to work for $13 per hour. This would be a deal, since he made $16 per hour at his last job. At the end of the conversation, he told the employer that he would work pushing a broom or be a relief man and work for less. (The employer did not go for this.)

One employer says when applicants come in to apply for a job at his store, he asks them if they can take a drug test today. The majority says, "Today is not a good day." That is a good way for the employer to weed out applicants who are not appropriate for hire. Some employers make prospective new employees pay for their own drug test. If they pass, they get hired and are reimbursed. Otherwise they may be out $85.

This same employer had a man in his thirties training from an R.O.P. program, and he planned to hire him because he worked so hard. Toward the end of his training, he stopped coming to work and to class. He never called the employer or the instructor and just disappeared. The employer stated, "This is definitely a new society."

One student was placed in an office and she quit after six hours. She said, "It was too hard." All she had to do was make phone calls and take messages.

A college placement specialist had a student who needed a job, the prospective employee told the specialist she wanted a job where she could sit and do her homework.

One high school student did her training phase at a veterinary hospital; she wanted to quit after her third day because the cleaning supplies were making her ill. Little did she know she was being let go due to her poor attitude, calling out the day after Thanksgiving and because she used someone's computer to play online.

I met with a retail-clothing employer at the beginning of 2007. She told me she asked an applicant for her street address, and the applicant's response was Niqually and Sixth Street. The seventeen-year-old applicant had to call home to get her street address. She even left out the "s" in Nisqually. This same employer was in need of an assistant manager, but she had not been able to find anyone who wanted to work or take on the responsibility. I shared this job with a friend of mine who knew someone who wanted a job in customer service. When my friend telephoned the potential applicant, her response was that she did not want to work weekends. This employer said people want a paycheck but they don't want to work.

In the spring of 2007, I called one of my R.O.P. students at home to remind him that I still needed his medical emergency information for our work-training program. The student then put his mother on the phone. She was very snippy with me and asked why I was calling on a Saturday. I told her because it was my job. It took weeks to obtain the information. In addition, he dropped the class prior to going to work.

The problem with today's work ethics and generation seems to be based on worldviews, demographics, and economics. With our children, students, and applicants, we may need to teach to their strengths. In addition, we need to provide constant reinforcement and positive feedback.

On a more positive note: We had one graduate who spent a lot of time watching television and playing on his computer. It was very difficult to get him motivated, even though he had very supportive parents. To make a long story short, he finally went to the California Conservation Corps.

We had a student who was put to work three different times through a work-training program and was never hired. She lived with her dad and siblings, and no one in her family worked. Therefore, there were no role models and no motivation. After many conversations and great perseverance, she finally went into the California Conservation Corps. There are many who learn from their past mistakes on job sites and later become successful. That is what counts!

> **"Success is not final, failure is not fatal: it is the courage to continue that counts."**
> **(Sir Winston Churchill)**

WORKER RIGHTS AND ETHICS
WORKERS HAVE RIGHTS

Sometimes employees may be taken advantage of by their employers and not be aware of it. Here are some examples of how employees may be mistreated on their job sites:

- Some employees are asked to clock out and then clock back in.

- Not having a work permit on the job site.

- Sometimes not providing back braces for heavy lifting.

- Being asked to do things that they should not be doing, such as operating machinery, serving alcohol, or using certain equipment while underage.

- Not being aware of safety issues.

- Not providing employees with safety equipment for the job.

- Not being appropriately trained on the job.

- Employers not following the labor laws.

- Not giving their employees breaks.

- Working overtime and not getting paid for it.

- Being paid under the table.

- Some employers only hire girls.

- Some employers hire or don't hire based on sex, race, or age.

- Some employers may take back your paycheck stubs and give you cash.

- Many high school students under the age of eighteen are working more hours than they are allowed to work.

All minors age twelve to seventeen must have a "permit to work," which must be on the job site. Work permits are issued by the schools. Every time you change jobs until you reach the age of eighteen, you will need a work permit. Students may check with their work-experience coordinators at their schools for hours and procedures on working.

Some fryers in restaurants do not have hoods, and that causes a safety issue. Sometimes you may be scheduled to come in and work, then are sent home because business is too slow. So they end up not paying you for that day. According to the labor laws, you have the right to be paid every time your employer asks you to report to work.

Employers do not all know the law, and some choose to ignore it. Therefore, it is vitally important for new hires to know the labor laws.

Your rights as a worker are enforced and protected by the California Department of Industrial Relations, Division of Labor Standards Enforcement.

The following are some of your rights that protect your working conditions:

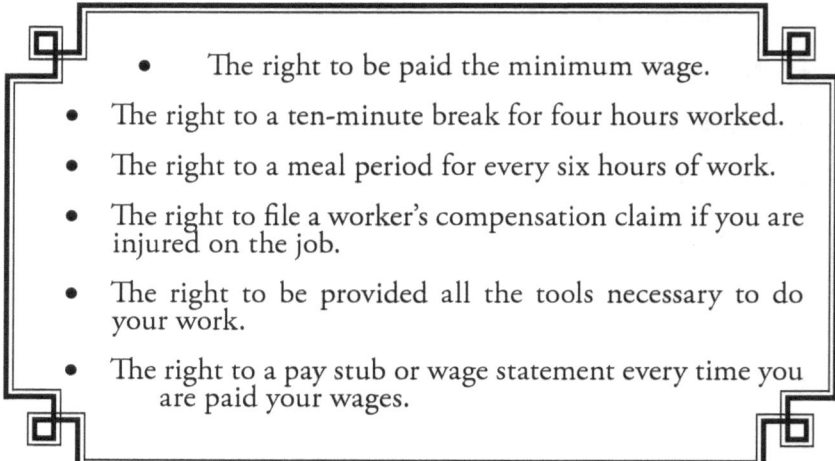

- The right to be paid the minimum wage.
- The right to a ten-minute break for four hours worked.
- The right to a meal period for every six hours of work.
- The right to file a worker's compensation claim if you are injured on the job.
- The right to be provided all the tools necessary to do your work.
- The right to a pay stub or wage statement every time you are paid your wages.

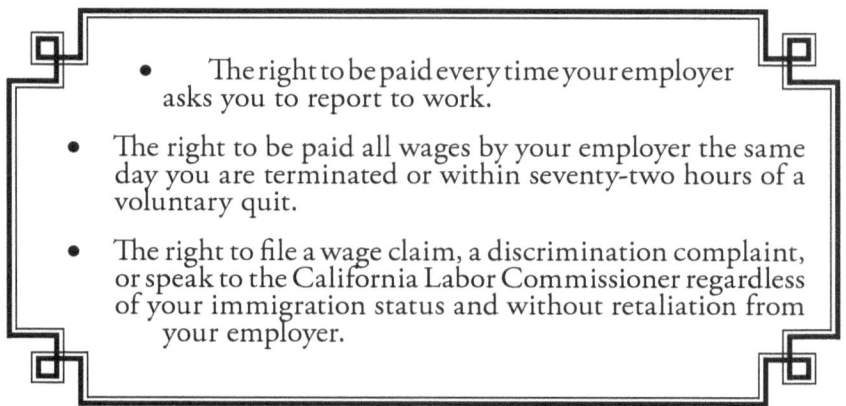

- The right to be paid every time your employer asks you to report to work.

- The right to be paid all wages by your employer the same day you are terminated or within seventy-two hours of a voluntary quit.

- The right to file a wage claim, a discrimination complaint, or speak to the California Labor Commissioner regardless of your immigration status and without retaliation from your employer.

If you feel you are being mistreated, make sure to document everything and take the appropriate actions. See numbers and Web sites below:

The California Division of Labor Standards Enforcement / Los Angeles (213) 620-6330

320 West Fourth Street, Suite 450, CA 90013

Cal/OSHA 1-800-963-9424

Minimum wage: 1-888-275-9243 (Ask Wage)

Prevailing wage hotline: (415) 703-4774

California labor laws can be found by contacting the Division of Labor Standards Enforcement (DSLE) offices or by visiting the Web sites.

www.dir.ca.gov

www.workitout.ca.gov

1905 MODEL F FORD TOURING CAR

GENERATION X & Y

CHAPTER NINE

What is Generation X & Y? Could this be a possible answer to our generation gap? I am not an expert on this topic, but do encourage you to read up on some of the findings on this subject if it is in your interest. I do find it very fascinating, because it may define how some of us are the way we are, and our work ethics. This may be due to the timeframe we were born into and what events transpired in those years. I also believe when things happen to us such as abuse, death in the family, accidents, hardships, poverty, and tragic events, etc., it plays a huge role on our character and who we become. Even winning the lottery changes your life. Of course, being born into the Bill Gates family or other wealthy people defines who you are and who you may become. Future events may continue to define our future generations. This could become Generation Z. Then what about the later years? Only time and our new generations to come will tell.

People who do not believe in God often say, "How do you know he exists if you have never seen him?" I used to say to my son, "Just because you don't see it, does not mean it is not there." So, just because I was not present when Jesus was on the Earth does not mean he wasn't. Just because I was not here during the Great Depression and the other historic events does not mean they did not happen.

In comparison to today, I could consider myself being raised somewhat poor, yet our needs were always met. My grandparents raised me for the first eight years of my life. They taught me how to value and appreciate things, which my parents later reinforced. Of course, people who were raised before me did not have the things that I had. We can trace history and go back as far as the time when people rode horses and there were no cars. In earlier times, there were donkeys and camels to ride and people walked from city to city. How about the Pony Express for your mail? People who were born in the '20s, '30s, and '40s who are still alive have some real stories to tell.

"I am not here by chance, but by God's choosing to fulfill his special purpose for this generation." (Roy Lessin)

When I was a teen living at home in Hacienda Heights, California, a friend of mine and I were out in the backyard one afternoon and above our heads we saw a spaceship/flying saucer go by. We did not tell anyone, because they would have thought we were on drugs. There are many things that people see, hear, and experience that some of us just might not believe. We each have a measure of faith. It is up to us what we choose to believe.

Our generation today does not understand how we survived without the Internet, digital cameras, DVDs, cell phones, iPods, etc. Our present and future generation may not be able to relate to all the past events in history that have occurred.

Just to name a few for example:

- The Gulf War

- The demise of the Berlin Wall

- Desert Storm

- The 1986 *Challenger* explosion

- Major earthquakes

- Hurricane Andrew in 1992

- Rodney King and the 1992 Los Angeles riots

- The O.J. Simpson murder trial

- The Oklahoma City bombing

- The death of Princess Diana

- Elvis Presley, his musical influence and his death

- The death of Mother Teresa 1997

- The Lewinsky scandal surrounding former president Clinton

- The Columbine shootings

- Woodstock '99

- The AIDS epidemic

- The Y2K bug

- September 11, 2001, the New York Twin Towers attack

- The global war on terror

- The war in Iraq

- The West Nile Virus outbreak

- The SARS epidemic in 2003

- The bird flu/mad cow disease

- The major hurricanes, like the Indian Ocean tsunami disaster/ Katrina in 2005

- Virginia Tech. Shootings 4/07

- Major Fires 10/07 & the list continues

We can go back as far as early civilization for events that no one alive today witnessed; like Adam & Eve, Noah's Arc with the great flood, Moses and the Ten Commandments, Jesus and prophets walking the Earth. Earlier presidents, writing of the U.S. Constitution, the Declaration of Independence, Hitler, slavery, Martin Luther King and so on, are just a few more examples of historical events. So, just because we were not there or born yet, does not mean it didn't take place. All these events have major impacts in the world and in people's lives.

As most of us know:

- The 1920s were called the Roaring '20s.

- The '30s was the Great Depression.

- The '40s was World War II, women entering the workplace.

- The '50s was the baby boom, sock hop dances, bomb shelters, and thousands of servicemen came back to America from World War II. Bread was fourteen cents a loaf.

- The '60s was the hippies social revolution/the youth age; Elvis returned to music from the service. Minimum wage was $1.

- The '70s was the Vietnam War, the disco era, and the women's movement. Bread was twenty-four cents a loaf.

- The '80s was the MTV generation and the me, me, me generation of status-seekers. Pop rock, new wave, punk, country, rap, and hip hop music became popular. Rap actually became popular in the late '80s and continued its popularity through today.

- The '90s was the decade of violence and technology. It was the merger decade and the electronic age. In 1992, the World Wide Web was born. Minimum wage was $5.15 and later went to $6.75.

- 2000, the Y2K bug, the new millennium, war, terror, epidemics, and disasters.

- 2001 – New silent generation and global warming.

- 2006 Average price for a loaf of bread is $1.98. Whole-wheat bread costs between $0.78 and $3.38. This all varies depending on the type of bread and where you purchased it.

- 2007 the minimum wage increases to $7.50 and in 2008 another increase to $8.00.

- 5/07 the price of supreme gas rose to $3.89 per gallon and continues to rise and fluctuate.

So what is X and Y, and are there any future letters to come? Research shows that Generation X is considered to be the people who were born approximately in the early 1960s, or 1964 to about 1976. Those born in the late '70s to about the year 2001 are known as Generation Y. The baby boomer generation was born between 1946 and 1964. When I researched the years, there was no real precise definition for some of the years. These dates were as close as I could find and they varied somewhat within a few years. What did we call past generations? See the section on the American generation in chapter twelve.

Based on research defining Generation X and Y, demographers have usually relied on the formative experiences of national events to characterize the generation groups. As the years have been defined, it shows that my son and I were born in two different generations. This may explain why in his teen years, we just did not see eye to eye.

Some of the crazes and events my son and I went through together while I was raising him are:

- Teddy Ruxpin, the Cabbage Patch Kids, the Care Bears, the Smurfs

- Guns N' Roses, Vanilla Ice, and MC Hammer in the late 1980s

- Mutant Ninja Turtles

- the game and collection of pogs

- the Power Rangers, *Barney & Friends*

- the Tickle Me Elmo craze in 1996, the Pokémon craze

- the ever-popular TV show *The Simpsons*

- the skateboard/scooter

- all the different types of music genres

- Bill Gates and Microsoft, the World Wide Web

- video games such as Nintendo, Sega Genesis, Super Nintendo, Nintendo 64, Game Boy, Sony Play Station, Play Station 2. After my son moved out came the following:

- stem cell research/cloning, gay marriages, and hybrid cars

- the X-Box, then Play Station 3, the Nintendo Wii, and the iPods

How many of our kids had all of those "toys"? One of these was always on my son's Christmas list. Now we have plasma televisions. Summer of 2007 came the iPhone, the size of a cell phone. It has a keyboard and wireless Internet. People were standing in line to buy this new device for $600, depending on where you purchase it. The list goes on, and will continue to grow with the continued demand, population, and technology. At what point will our needs be met to stop being competitive? Everything new is not better for all of us.

When I grew up in the early 1960s, we grew up with *Bonanza, Flipper,* and *Lassie* for our television entertainment. Later it became Hobo Kelly with her big glasses and then came Bozo the clown, *I Love Lucy,* and *Happy Days.* As I got older, the words in the music we listened to were understandable and we could sing to it. There was no profanity. Now there are a lot of oldies but goodies. I began listening to Nancy Sinatra, ("These Boots Are Made for Walking") and to Karen Carpenter songs. Later it was the Rolling Stones, the Beatles, Elvis, the Eagles, Foreigner, Heart, Led Zeppelin, Pink Floyd, Bob Seger, Fleetwood Mac, Queen, etc. When I was sixteen, we had the concerts California Jam. I didn't get into country until I became an adult. I believe that country music is much better now than it was when I was growing up. I am sure this will take some of you back in time.

When I was younger, I despised classical music because it put me to sleep. Now I enjoy listening to Yanni. I listened to records, eight-track tapes in the car, cassette tapes; now we have CDs and DVDs. What comes next?

My son David, who is now in his mid-twenties, used to listen to rap music and songs with vulgarity in the lyrics. I am now happy and surprised to say he is listening to the old songs I used to listen to, such as the ones listed above.

Also, as I was growing up, my generation was mostly into drinking, smoking cigarettes, marijuana, cocaine, and a few of the other drugs we won't mention. None of that has changed. Eric Clapton wrote a song called "Cocaine." It makes me wonder how that influenced my generation! Of course now we have the date-rape drug and ecstasy. It has been said, "The Y Generation is one of the most medicated generations in human history." That is scary. This is largely due to all the prescriptions, antidepressants, behavior-altering drugs, pain medications, etc.

Using work ethics as a guide, maybe we need to understand into which generation we are born and learn to adapt, and accept the fact that we truly are all unique. As we know, not everyone responds the same way and not everyone is motivated the same way. We all come from various backgrounds and different cultures. There are many references, resources, workshops, and trainings available to assist those who may want to better understand, learn, or adapt with our different generations and its workforce.

So, are you an X, Y, or Z? Or are you in the past generation, the me generation, or the last generation?

> **"All the world is a stage, and all men and women are merely players."**
> **(William Shakespeare)**

A POEM FOR COMPUTER USERS OVER 40!

A computer was something on TV.

From a science fiction show of note.

A window was something you hated to clean.

And ram was the father of a goat.

Meg was the name of my girlfriend.

And gig was a job for the nights.

Now they all mean different things.

And that really mega bites.

An application was for employment.

A program was a TV show.

A cursor used profanity.

A keyboard was a piano.

A memory was something that you lost with age.

A CD was a bank account.

And if you had a 3-inch floppy.

You hoped nobody found out.

Compress was something you did to the garbage.

Not something you did to a file.

And if you unzipped anything in public.

You'd be in jail for a while.

Log-on was adding wood to the fire.

Hard drive was a long trip on the road.

A mouse pad was where a mouse lived.

And a backup happened to your commode.

Cut you did with a pocket-knife.

Paste you did with glue.

A web was a spider's home.

And a virus was the flu.

I guess I'll stick to my pad and paper.

And the memory in my head.

I hear nobody's been killed in a computer crash.

But when it happens they wish they were dead.

(Anonymous)

LEADING A MULTI-GENERATIONAL WORKFORCE

CHAPTER TEN

By Joanne Sujansky, Ph.D. / Printed by Permission of KEY Group.

"Generational differences represent a critical new aspect to workplace diversity."

Effectively motivating and training employees from various generations requires understanding the perspectives of each age group. As "Generation Y" enters the workforce in increasing numbers, managers need to know more about the expectations these young people bring to the job.

Before making assumptions about employee retention based on past experience, consider that you are about to see a new wave of employees with a whole new set of expectations swarm the workplace. Known as Generation Y, they might have a few traits that will surprise even the seasoned manager. Many organizations have likely already conquered the management challenges posed by traditionalists, baby boomers, and Generation X workers, and have discovered how to motivate and retain those valuable employees through some of the more prosperous economic times that we've seen. But with the arrival of Generation Y, managers will need a whole new set of rules.

Generation Y has been entering the workforce since 1998 and will continue to do so in burgeoning numbers. While there are approximately 75 million traditionalists, 76 million baby boomers, and 44 million Generation X members, Generation Y is closer to 80 million, and we have not even begun to reach critical mass in the workforce yet. Managers need to prepare for the unique requirements of Generation Y and the potential clash with the other groups as they mix in the workplace.

To begin with, it is helpful to understand the environment that shaped each group. With this information, you can then adopt an innovative management style, motivate them to work together, and minimize conflict among the different generations.

WHAT SHAPED THEM

Born before 1945, traditionalists were influenced by the Great Depression and World War II. After the war, this generation rebuilt America by having faith in and partnering with institutions. In doing so, they displayed a strong work ethic and fueled the economic boom. Fifty percent of traditionalist men are war veterans.

Born between 1946 and 1964, baby boomers grew up in optimistic times of expansion, watching and living *Happy Days*. They had great expectations for them. Where their parents fought wars abroad and came home victorious, boomers fought for their glory at work.

Generation X was born between 1965 and 1976. They experienced economic difficulties during the '90s, just as they were entering the workforce. Many were forced to take temporary work, wait tables, and accept jobs outside of their area of study in college. Because Generation X came of age during a bleak job market, soaring national debt, the Gulf War, and lack of opportunities, the harsh economic realities of the time shaped their worldview. They come to their positions of responsibility with the knowledge that there are no guarantees.

Generation Y was born between 1977 and 1994. They grew up in a time of economic expansion and unprecedented prosperity, and until now have never experienced a downturn. Those in this generation have seen more at an earlier age than most in previous generations, such as chilling footage of the Oklahoma City bombing, the Columbine shootings, and the tragedy of September 11. Exposure to these events through twenty-four-hour media has brought the world instantly to them. Because this techno-savvy generation has "seen" the world, it has a more global perspective and expanded definition of diversity than previous generations.

So is the generation gap back? You bet! In fact, generational differences represent a critical new aspect to workplace diversity. At no other time in history have organizations been faced with four generations of employees working together, each with very different values, attitudes, and expectations. But the differences that separate these generations do not have to result in conflict and lost productivity. Following are suggestions for leading all three groups successfully.

OFFER CHOICES

While different, Generation X and Generation Y have some similarities. Both will demand a more innovative workplace, with flexible hours, state-of-the art resources, cooperative scheduling, and supervisors who listen. They expect many choices, along with the freedom to pursue them. Both want to build a portfolio of skills and are committed to career development. They won't work any other way and will continue to negotiate a work-life balance—something the traditionalists and boomers may not require as many choices, make the same options available to them as you do to the other generations. The two older generations value inclusion, and keeping them "in the loop" with the younger generations will likely enhance their productivity.

OFFER TRAINING OPPORTUNITIES

To retain employees of all generations, it is important to appeal to their desire to learn. Emphasize career growth, paid training, and skill development. Ask what matters to them, and really listen to their answers. Smart managers can best learn to deal with the different groups, and to negotiate through potential areas of friction between the generations, by assuming the role of coach when dealing with their employees. When using the coaching method, balance corrective feedback with praise. Catch them doing something right, and reward them for it. Though effective in the past, the traditional "I tell/you do" school of management may not work with Generation X and Generation Y. One of the reasons Generation X and Y will be so valuable is that there will be a shortage of skilled managers to replace the retiring traditionalists and boomers. Developing experienced and skilled young managers will become vital to any organization hoping to compete in the future.

Offer an Evolving Workplace

Because the incoming group of Gen Y employees will be so large, the workplace will have to change to accommodate their unique attributes. Leaders have to evolve as well. They will have to be creative in developing new motivational techniques if they want to retain their employees and obtain the highest performance and output possible. Managers must be innovative to retain the best people.

To manage Gen Y employees, it is important to take advantage of their strengths, and help them to understand their weaknesses. While traditionalists and boomers may be content to "wait their turn," Gen X and Gen Y demand a relationship-intensive environment with a lot of one-on-one communication and timely feedback on their performance. Managers have also found that X's and Y's expect that everyone in the office will make adaptations for the good of the team. This can sometimes cause conflicts with the older traditionalists and boomer generations.

Build a Successful Multi-Generational Environment

To enhance the work environment, recognize that these groups will have different perspectives, and respect that generations differ in the way they see the world. It will be necessary to implement and reward collaborative activities with a multi-disciplinary approach. When you employ a coaching style of management, you will be able to give regular feedback to your employees, and you will also receive the information you need from them to know what is working. This will benefit the relationships among all your employees and go a long way toward retaining your best team members.

About the Author:

Dr. Joanne G. Sujansky, CSP (Certified Speaking Professional) has over twenty-five years of experience helping leaders increase organizational growth and profitability by creating and sustaining what she calls a "vibrant entrepreneurial organization." She is an international keynote speaker, founder of KEY Group, and the author of numerous books on leadership, change, and retention. A member of the National Speakers Association, she holds their highest earned designation, Certified Speaking Professional. Reach Dr. Sujansky at (800) 456-5790 or at: www.joannesujansky.com.

CONCLUSION
CHAPTER ELEVEN

When most of us went to school, we did not have all the work-experience training programs and resources to help us like there are now. It seems today more people are being placed or referred to jobs by someone else, more than people who are actually getting their own jobs. This is due to all the wonderful programs and agencies that are helping people go to work. Many times after being put to work by someone or a program, prospective employees find themselves needing another job; they say they can't find one. This often happens when people are put to work and not shown how to actually seek employment and what tools are needed.

Before I ever put anyone to work, I teach him or her how to get a job. I teach people how to dress, fill out an application, go on interviews, write a résumé, and some basic work ethics. After that, it is up to them. I strongly believe all those who put students and adults to work should teach those basic fundamentals. I also know that many programs do and many applicants are very successful. However, some applicants just don't listen or care. There is an old famous Chinese proverb that says, **"Give a man a fish and you feed him for a day. Teach a man to fish and you feed him for a lifetime."**

Personally, I believe there should be some kind of mandatory boot camp before leaving high school, along with a class that teaches students the tools they will need to get a job and live on their own. If a semester of military training would be mandatory for all to graduate, they would get the structure and discipline they so desperately need. Think of how different our world/ society would be and become!

What if we looked at the possibility of taking gang members and/or prisoners and placing them on the front lines of our military? This would allow them to act out their anger and violent behaviors for the good of our nation! Many of our prisons are overcrowded, and often when the prisoners are released, they return. Think of the powerful force and impact we would have in the war against terror.

I get so many job leads every week and have developed a job hotline list along with a one-page recipe on how to find a job. I distribute and pass these out continuously. There are so many businesses that take applications on a regular basis and many hire routinely.

There are ongoing job fairs, so check with your local cities and colleges. When you attend job fairs, make sure to bring your résumé, a sample application, and **"always dress to impress."**

The resources are available to those who want to work. People should keep in mind that every job is a stepping-stone to another. Stop waiting for your dream job to knock on your door before you go to work. Get a job now, obtain some experience, get some money in your pocket, and keep searching on your days off for what you really want. In the meantime, you will be building your reference base and will find out what you enjoy doing and not enjoy doing.

Many young adults who have gone into the California Conservation Corps, Job Corps, and military have totally transformed their lives.

From what I have observed, most people want a job but do not really want to work. The ones who want to work are working. I believe if anyone wants a job badly enough and is able to work, they will obtain a job. There is someone hiring every day!

If you or anyone you know needs a job, please refer them to my other book on *Robin's Simple Recipe for Finding a Job!*

> **"More of our basic human needs will be simultaneously satisfied through work then by any other arena of our lives."**
> **(Sigmund Freud)**

AMERICAN GENERATIONS

CHAPTER TWELVE

Ref: (Wikipedia)

TERM	**PERIOD**
Awakening Generation	1701 – 1723
First Great Awakening	1730 – 1740
Liberty Generation	1724 – 1741
Republican Generation	1742 – 1766
Compromise Generation	1767 – 1791
Second Great Awakening	1790 – 1840
Transcendentalist Generation	1789 – 1819
Transcendental Generation	1792 – 1821
Abolitionist Generation	1819 – 1842
Gilded Generation	1822 – 1842

Progressive Generation	1843 – 1859
Missionary Awakening	1886 – 1908
Missionary Generation	1860 – 1882
Lost Generation	1883 – 1900
Interbellum Generation	1900 – 1910
G.I. Generation	1900 – 1924
Greatest Generation	1911 – 1924
American High	1929 – 1956
Silent Generation	1925 – 1945
Baby Boomers	1946 – 1964
Beat Generation	1948 - 1962
Generation Jones	1954 - 1965
Consciousness Revolution	1964 – 1984
Baby Busters	1958 – 1968
Generation X	1961 – 1981
MTV Generation	1975 – 1985
Culture Wars	1984 - 2005
Boomerang Generation	1981 – 1986
Generation Y	1977 – 2003
iGeneration	1982 –
New Silent Generation	2001 –
The Millennials?	2007 -

BELOIT COLLEGE, WISCONSIN

Printed by Permission

Just in case you weren't feeling too old today, this will certainly change things. Each year, the staff at Beloit College in Wisconsin put together a list to try to give the faculty a sense of the mindset of that year's incoming freshmen.

Here is a former list:

The people who are starting college this fall across the nation were born in 1982:

- They have no meaningful recollection of the Reagan Era and probably did not know he had ever been shot.

- They were prepubescent when the Persian Gulf War was waged.

- Black Monday 1987 is as significant to them as the Great Depression.

- They were eleven when the Soviet Union broke apart and do not remember the Cold War.

- They have never feared a nuclear war.

- They are too young to remember the space shuttle blowing up.

- Tiananmen Square means nothing to them.

- Their lifetime has always included AIDS.

- Bottle caps have always been screw off and plastic.

FEELING OLD YET? IT GETS BETTER

- Atari predates them, as do vinyl albums. The expression,

"You sound like a broken record" means nothing to them.

- They have never owned a record player.

- They have likely never played Pac Man and have never heard of Ping-Pong.

- They may have never heard of an eight-track. The compact disc was introduced when they were one year old.

- As far as they know, stamps have always cost about 33 cents.

- They have always had an answering machine.

- Most have never seen a TV set with only thirteen channels, nor have they seen a black-and-white TV.

- They have always had cable.

- There has always been VCRs, but they have no idea what BETA is.

- They cannot fathom not having a remote control.

- They were born the year that Walkmen were introduced by Sony.

- "Roller skating" has always meant inline for them.

- Jay Leno has always been on *The Tonight Show*.

- They have no idea when or why Jordache jeans were cool.

- Popcorn has always been cooked in the microwave.

- They have never seen Larry Bird play.

- They never took a swim and thought about *Jaws*.

- The Vietnam War is as ancient history to them as WWI, WWII, and the Civil War.

- They have no idea that Americans were ever held hostage in Iran.

- They can't imagine what hard contact lenses are.

- They don't know who Mork was or where he was from.

FEELING LIKE A REFUGEE FROM A GERIATRIC WARD YET?

- They never heard: "Where's the beef?" "I'd walked a mile for a Camel," or "De plane, de plane!"

- They do not care who shot J.R. (and have no idea who J.R. is).

- The *Titanic* was found? They thought we always knew where it was.

- Michael Jackson has always been white.

- Kansas, Chicago, Boston, America, and Alabama are places, not groups.

- McDonald's never came in Styrofoam containers.

- There has always been MTV.

- They don't have a clue how to use a typewriter.

Do you feel old yet? Pass this on to the other old fogies in your life.

Ladies and gentlemen, I give you the class of 2000.

TREATING CUSTOMERS WELL

PROPER CUSTOMER TREATMENT

Being polite to a customer is very important. There are at least four ways to be polite to customers:

1. Use a customer's name, if you know it.

2. Call a woman "miss" or "ma'am;" call a man "sir."

3. Say "excuse me" to get the attention of a customer.

4. Find out what the customer wants to know. If you do not know the answer to a customer's question, do not say, "I don't know." Tell the customer, "I'm sorry; I do not know, but I will find out for you."

ASSISTING CUSTOMERS

Most customers enjoy courteous and respectful service. There are times when additional assistance may be needed by a specific customer. Always ask, "May I help you?" Be sure to wait for an answer before assisting a customer.

Some customers who may need extra help could be senior citizens, parents with babies or small children, disabled individuals, or non-English-speaking persons.

Treating customers well is an important part of any business. Below are some suggestions to help assist customers.

HELPING AN OLDER CUSTOMER

Some older people may not see or hear as well as you do. Some are not very strong. Not all older people have these problems. You will have to pay attention to older customers to see if they need your help.

Some suggestions to assist a senior citizen may be to:

1. Offer to write things down if they are hard to remember.

2. Open a door for them.

3. Offer to read signs and menus.

4. Talk slowly and clearly to ensure that the customer hears you.

5. Offer to carry heavy bags or packages.

HELPING PARENTS WITH BABIES OR SMALL CHILDREN

Fathers and mothers with babies or small children may need extra help. They have their hands full!

Some suggestions to help you assist parents may be to:

1. Open a door for them.

2. Carry bags or packages.

3. Complete the transaction as quickly as possible.

HELPING A DISABLED PERSON

A customer on crutches, or using some other type of assistive device, may need help getting through a door or finding a place to sit in a crowded restaurant. A customer who puts crutches aside to sit down will want to have the crutches close by. Never take a customer's crutches away unless the person asks you to do so. People using wheelchairs sometimes cannot reach things; offer assistance to a person using a wheelchair before actually assisting.

Some suggestions to assist disabled customers:

1. Offer to open a door for them.

2. Ask them if they would like your help to read signs and menus.

3. Talk slowly and clearly. Do not yell.

4. Offer to carry heavy bags or packages.

5. Put change carefully in the person's hand.

6. Tell the person what you are doing.

HELPING INDIVIDUALS WHO DO NOT SPEAK ENGLISH

Give extra time to customers who do not speak fluent English. Be patient and do your best to understand what the customer is saying. Most people can understand more of a foreign language than they can speak.

Some suggestions for assisting non-English-speaking persons may be to:

1. Speak clearly and smile.

2. Gesture when necessary.

THE ANGRY CUSTOMER

Every person on the job runs into an angry customer once in a while. Here are some guidelines to follow when a customer gets upset:

1. Listen to what the customer is saying.

2. Say you are sorry. Even if the problem is not your fault, you should say you are sorry that it happened.

3. Explain why the problem might have happened. When the customer knows the reason for the problem, he or she might cool off.

4. Try to solve the problem. If you are not sure you can solve the problem, go to your supervisor and ask for help.

5. Contact your boss right away if the customer is very angry.

6. **Above all, stay cool yourself.**

Recreated / Printed by Permission / Partners & Education /Youth Programs, Poway Unified School District.

The Big Five

a.k.a. Quality Customer Service Determinants

Empathy

Willingness and readiness to help

Probe customers' needs

Care

Explain in understandable terms

Pleasant manner

Responsiveness

Make eye contact

Use friendly body language

Show interest

Give correct information

Give prompt service

Properly complete all transactions

ASSURANCE

Offer personalized attention

- Be friendly

- Be courteous

- Greet them cordially

- Use the customer's name

- Say "thank you."

- Maintain confidentiality

Have the ability to communicate job knowledge

Speak clearly

Use a pleasant and sure tone of voice

RELIABILITY

Be accurate

Be sympathetic and reassuring when customers have problems

Follow through on commitments

TANGIBLES

Professional appearance

- Neat attire

- No gum chewing, smoking, eating, or drinking in public work areas

- **Wear your name badges**
- **Be organized**
- **Maintain neat work areas that are well-stocked**

(Anonymous)

QUALITIES OF A LEADER

**"A great leader's courage to fulfill his vision comes from passion, not position."
(John Maxwell)**

1. A leader is always full of praise.

2. A leader learns to use the phrase "thank you" and "please" on his way to the top.

3. A leader is always growing.

4. A leader is possessed with his dreams.

5. A leader launches forth before success is certain.

6. A leader is not afraid of confrontation.

7. A leader talks about his own mistakes before talking about someone else's.

8. A leader is a person of honesty and integrity.

9. A leader has a good name.

10. A leader makes others better.

11. A leader is quick to praise and encourages the smallest amount of improvement.

12. A leader is genuinely interested in others.

13. A leader looks for opportunities to find someone doing something right.

14. A leader responds to his own failures and acknowledges them before others have to discover and reveal them.

15. A leader is specific in what he expects.

16. A leader takes others up with him.

17. A leader never allows murmuring from himself or others.

18. A leader is specific in what he expects.

19. A leader holds accountable those who work with him.

20. A leader does what is right rather than what is popular.

21. A leader is a servant.

(Anonymous)

ANOTHER APPROACH:
THE INFORMATIONAL
INTERVIEW

The best way to find out about a job or career area in which you are interested is to talk to the people who are actually doing the job—or even better, to talk to the person who hires those people. This method of employer contact, called "the informational interview," can also be a very effective job-seeking method.

To arrange for an informational interview, call the personnel department of a company, and ask to talk with the person who hires workers in the area of your interest. Ask if you can set up an appointment to come in and talk with him or her for about fifteen minutes, at their convenience. Explain that you are thinking about going into that type of work someday, and would like to know more about the work, as well as what kind of training, experience, and personality characteristics the employer looks for.

REMEMBER, you are seeking information; you are not interviewing for a job. You will be asking the questions of the employer, so you should be prepared. You should dress appropriately and act somewhat businesslike, as you will want to leave a positive impression with the employer. Be courteous and sensitive to the cues of the employer.

Do not take up too much of the employer's time, since they are doing you a favor by agreeing to talk with you. Most employers do not mind this type of request, and most feel flattered to have their advice sought.

When you have finished with your list of questions for the employer, thank him or her for the time. Do not offer a copy of your résumé. If the employer requests it, return with it at a later time. You do not want the employer to feel "tricked" into a job interview.

Sometimes, you may find out that you are already qualified for the job about which you are inquiring. An employer may request your résumé or suggest that you apply for a specific job. Employers sometimes suggest further contact and may even give you permission to use their name. These happenings would be extra benefits to your main goal of seeking "information," although some experts have speculated that doing information interviews actually more than doubles your job-seeking success.

Always be courteous and try to make a good impression. You never know when you may again encounter that employer as you are applying for jobs or even when you are working on a job. Finally, be certain to send the employer a brief letter thanking him or her for taking the time to talk to you.

SOURCES OF EMPLOYMENT

- ✔ Apprenticeship Programs
- ✔ Business Directories
- ✔ California Conservation Corps (C.C.C.)
- ✔ Canvassing
- ✔ Chambers of Commerce
- ✔ Civil Service Announcements
- ✔ Communications Media
- ✔ Employment Development Departments
- ✔ Industrial Parks
- ✔ Job Bulletin Boards
- ✔ Job Corps
- ✔ Job Fairs
- ✔ Local Newspapers
- ✔ Manufacturers or Distributors of Special Equipment
- ✔ Military Services
- ✔ Newspaper Advertisements
- ✔ Prior Employers and Employers to Whom Applications Are Made
- ✔ Private Employment Agencies
- ✔ Professional and Business Associations
- ✔ Radio, TV, Newspapers and Magazine Stories of New or Expanding Companies or Areas
- ✔ R.O.P. Training
- ✔ School Placement Services
- ✔ Suppliers, Customers, and Competitors of Prior Employers
- ✔ Teachers, Religious Advisors, Insurance Agents, Creditors, Bankers

- ✔ Trade Associations and Trade Publications
- ✔ Unions
- ✔ Friends, Relatives, and Neighbors
- ✔ Employment Web sites such as Monster.com
- ✔ Yellow Pages

" A GOOD PERCENTAGE OF JOBS ARE FILLED THROUGH NETWORKING."

MILITARY TRAINING PROGRAMS

Some students may need the guidance and discipline that the various branches of the Armed Forces can provide.

TECHNICAL SCHOOLS   The military technical schools are considered among the best in the world. They combine on-the-job training with excellent professional instruction. Many high school graduates are opting to develop skills in career fields of the future, rather than to attend college right away. Technical schools offer a good start for the career-building process. Experienced trainers in every job area provide practical, personalized training. And it is put to use right away in a job in the Armed Forces.

APPRENTICESHIP PROGRAMS   Some skills can lead to certification of completion of apprenticeship in jobs comparable to civilian fields trades in apprentice program, including carpenter, cement mason, commercial photographer, cook, machinist, maintenance mechanic, and power plant operator.

ENLISTED PROGRAMS   The Armed Forces are one of the largest employers and finest teachers of young people today. Men and women are assured of expert training for jobs matched to their abilities and interests in many skilled fields. For almost every job advertised in your local paper, there is a similar job in the Armed Forces.

The variety of jobs in the Armed Forces offer interesting work to suit all temperaments: outdoor or indoor; do-it-yourself; student; adventurer; and the person who seeks challenge and early leadership responsibilities. There's a place for all of them in the Armed Forces if they qualify.

Whatever skill field you choose, all Armed Forces personnel enjoy the same pay and promotion schedules, and great benefits unequaled in the civilian workforce. Among those benefits are:

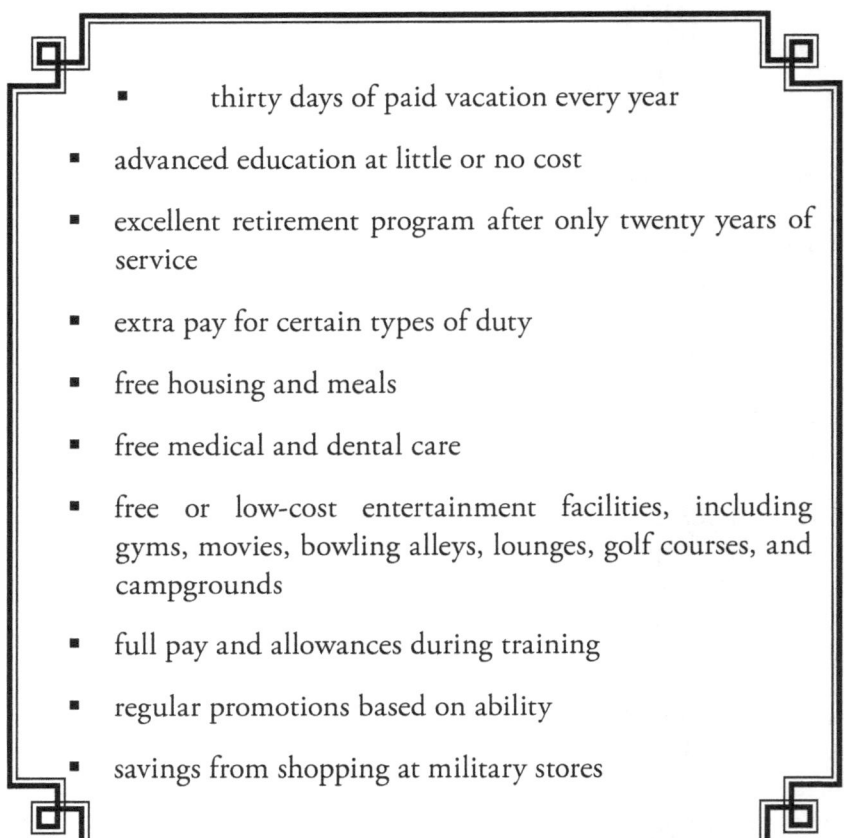

- thirty days of paid vacation every year
- advanced education at little or no cost
- excellent retirement program after only twenty years of service
- extra pay for certain types of duty
- free housing and meals
- free medical and dental care
- free or low-cost entertainment facilities, including gyms, movies, bowling alleys, lounges, golf courses, and campgrounds
- full pay and allowances during training
- regular promotions based on ability
- savings from shopping at military stores

In short, the Armed Forces gives young people a solid foundation for the future.

Printed by Permission/Partners & Education/Youth Programs/ Poway Unified School District.

ROBIN'S ONE-PAGE RECIPE FOR FINDING A JOB!

Apply where you want to work and keep on going back and keep on going back, to let them know you are interested in working there. Always dress to interview when you apply for a job and always go alone. Fill out your application neatly and completely, if something does not apply to you write, "N/A." Always use a black or blue pen, and take correction fluid or an erasable pen with you. You may attach a résumé to your application, and make sure to bring one to your interview.

When you turn in your application, ask for the manager so that you can introduce yourself. Shake their hand, smile, and show enthusiasm. Say, "Nice to meet you. I just wanted to give you my application and let you know that I am interested in working here." That is all you have to say. When you leave, write down where you went, the date, and the manager's name and what they said. Keep a log sheet of everywhere you go. When you go back to do your weekly or bi-weekly follow-up, you will know whom to ask for. If they tell you to come back on a certain day or time, make sure that you do. If they tell you to call on Tuesday at 4:00 and you don't, then that tells the employer that you do not want the job.

The more places that you go to apply and follow up on, the sooner you will get hired. Many times, you will be interviewed on the spot, so be prepared. The number-one question that is asked in interviews is "Tell me about yourself," so you need to be ready to talk about yourself. Let them know what your strengths are, what kind of person you are, and how you can fit in with their company. Work on your personal attributes; we all have them. Example: Look in the mirror every morning and start talking to yourself. Say whatever applies to you, such as, "I am a team player. I am organized, creative, and a fast learner. I am responsible, always take initiative, and have great time-management skills." Making personal confessions of your attributes will make you a more positive person and you will be able to sell yourself better in an interview. It will also help you to have a portfolio to bring with you to your interview.

Some of the things to put in your portfolio are:

Résumé, references, and recommendation letters

Certificates, awards, report cards, and transcripts

Vocational trainings, internships, R.O.P classes, and pictures of accomplishments

Outside activities, clubs, community service, etc.

You don't have a second chance to make a first impression!

Make sure you stay persistent and follow up!

If you are looking for a job and can't find one, you either don't know how to effectively search for a job or you are not motivated.

Remember to network, use all your resources, and attend job fairs. There are many services available that help people get jobs.

There is someone hiring every day!

Good luck!
R.L.R.

TEN MOST WANTED LIST

WHAT EMPLOYERS ARE LOOKING FOR!

Before you accept, evaluate the position carefully in terms of:

A HIGH SCHOOL DIPLOMA	When you tell an employer you stuck to it and got your high school diploma, you are saying you can stick to the job too. To an employer, a G.E.D. means you took the easy way out and may not last long on the job.
ABILITY TO PASS A DRUG TEST	Few employers will hire you without asking you to submit to a drug test. If you can't pass a pre-employment drug test, you fail—in life.
ABILITY TO PASS A CRIMINAL BACKGROUND CHECK	Even a minor shoplifting conviction can prevent you from landing an entry-level job for years to come. If you do have a police record to explain, be honest and tell the employer how the experience has changed you for the better.
A GOOD ATTITUDE	An employer wants people who have a positive attitude and outlook, someone who will contribute to a pleasant workplace. Show motivation, enthusiasm, and initiative. Go the extra mile!
BASIC COMPUTER SKILLS	Basic computer skills are easy to get and are required on most jobs today. Having even some computer skills will separate you from the crowd.

BASIC MATH SKILLS	Life is hard without basic math skills. You need to know how to read a ruler, how to add, subtract, multiply, and divide—and don't forget decimals and fractions. Without these skills, your climb to the top will be, shall we say, impossible.
GOOD COMMUNICATION SKILLS	When you talk to an employer, use a more formal approach and remember that the casual language you use with friends may be offensive to the boss. Make sure to have a professional voice mail message too!
NO VISIBLE TATTOOS OR BODY PIERCING	Since you don't know how your employer feels about tattoos and body piercings, cover them up if you can. Why take the chance of losing a good job over them?
ABILITY TO UNDERSTAND WRITTEN DIRECTIONS	If you have trouble with reading, get help. The ability to read well is the key to having a job that is going somewhere.
ABILITY TO WRITE	You may be the smartest person on the job, but if you can't spell or write a sentence, how will the employer know you are smart? Many employers will look at misspelled words on an application as an indication that a person won't be right for the job.
WORK ETHICS AND CUSTOMER SERVICE	Integrity, loyalty, honesty, responsibility, empathy, confidentiality, and respect are just some of the qualities required for success. "The Golden Rule": Treat others as you would like to be treated. (Anonymous) Has also been modified.

IF YOU'RE OFFERED THE JOB

**Before you accept, evaluate the position carefully
in terms of:**

Job Responsibility

WORKING HOURS

Pace of Work

Advancement
opportunities

SALARY RANGE

Benefits

Job Location

TRANSPORTATION
REQUIREMENTS—IS PUBLIC
TRANSPORT AVAILABLE OR DO
YOU NEED A CAR?

Working Conditions

Future possibilities—what
could the job lead to?

If you accept, you may want to write a confirmation note (even if you've accepted verbally). Make sure to confirm your starting date and time. Also know what the dress code is. Do not assume anything.

HOW TO KEEP YOUR JOB

Be Punctual

Always be on time or early. Call the employer if you will not be there or if you are late. Be responsible & show good work ethics, especially if you want to be promoted.

Show Initiative

Always be ready to find things to do or ask what else you can do. Look busy and always go the extra mile.

Be Aware of Safety Rules

Employers do not want to keep people who have accidents or who do not follow the safety rules. It is costly and dangerous to others.

Be a Team Player

Assist others; people depend on one another in work situations. Be able to work in a group, be goal oriented, have creative ideas, and exhibit integrity and leadership skills. Good communication is also essential. Remember: There is no "I" in team!

Be Enthusiastic

Always act like you enjoy your job. When you do, you become a more productive worker. Make sure to smile and focus on the positive.

Be Conscientious

Learn to be diligent, focused, avoid gossip, dress appropriately, and show appreciation for others. Do not come to work under the influence. Always use good judgment.

Be Respectful

If you do not like your job, look for something else on your days off. Make sure to always give two weeks' notice and give them a letter of resignation. In addition, ask for a letter of reference. Leave things in an organized manner for someone else.

Be Inquisitive

Take courses. Improve your methods. Make every effort to grow with your organization.

"People acting together as a group can accomplish things which no individual acting alone could ever hope to bring about."
Franklin Delano Roosevelt

"Unless you try to do something beyond what you have already mastered, you will never grow."
(Ralph Waldo Emerson)

Leaving Your Job?

- Don't just quit. Calm down and think it over.
- Make sure you have another job before you quit.
- Give a written notice to your employer FIRST.
- Complete all job responsibilities.
- Ask for a letter of reference or recommendation.
- Don't bad-mouth your employer.
- Don't brag about your new job to other employees.
- Do leave with good feelings.

Recreated & printed with permission, Partners & Education/Youth Programs/ Poway Unified School District

THE ABCs OF
LOVING YOUR JOB

I've discovered that loving the job you have, or finding a job you can love, is dependent on three things. Dr. John C. Maxwell calls these "The ABCs of loving your job."

Printed with permission. *By Dr. John C. Maxwell*

ASSOCIATES: Work with people you enjoy.

For years, I have bragged about my staff. I realize that not everyone is surrounded with my kind of staff. The good news is you can develop one. When I talk to leaders about hiring people, I advise them to hire first for affinity, second for **character**, and third for **specific skills**. If you bring on someone you like whom you can trust, you can teach him or her whatever skills they need for the job.

Regarding your existing staff, don't forget that people skills can be learned as well. If you are willing to make the investment, you can cultivate the right kind of people that everyone wants to be around.

BELIEF: *Trust that your work is worthwhile and making a vital difference.*

Bob Buford has written that many people spend the first half of their career pursuing success. When success alone is found to be lacking, they give the second half to the pursuit of significance, which is far more satisfying.

If your job is not making a difference in this world, by all means, get out there and find something else. But in many situations, you'll find a sense of making a difference through your work if you simply look for it.

CHALLENGE: *Find a job big enough to let you keep growing for the rest of your life.*

Like shoes that are too small pinch the feet, a job that is too small pinches a leader's spirit. If the job you have now offers no opportunity to grow, decide to grow anyway. Invest in your own personal development, sharpening leadership skills, interpersonal skills, and technical skills. What you'll discover is that your organization will find a place for a person who has made a priority out of growth. And if they don't, the competition will! And keep this in mind when you consider your top performers. Are you providing room for your top performers to grow? If you don't, someone else will.

Finding joy in your work, or evaluating a lack of joy, can be achieved by considering associates, beliefs, and challenges.

John C. Maxwell is an internationally recognized leadership expert, speaker, and author who has sold more than 12 million books. His organizations have trained more than 1 million leaders worldwide. Dr. Maxwell is the founder of INJOY Stewardship Services and EQUIP.

100 WAYS
TO MOTIVATE YOURSELF

1.	Create a vision	26.	Act like a hero
2.	Tell a true lie	27.	Accept your willpower
3.	Leave your comfort zone	28.	Say no to yourself
4.	Find out your key	29.	Make new word connections
5.	Plan your work	30.	De-program yourself
6.	Move your goal post	31.	Open the present
7.	Dribble with another hand	32.	Serve and grow rich
8.	Play your character	33.	Imitate Columbo
9.	Sit quietly	34.	Give away some power
10.	Use the right chemicals	35.	Talk to yourself
11.	Leave high school	36.	Schedule your comebacks
12.	Lose face	37.	Live your true life
13.	Sing without feeling	38.	Get up on the right side of the bed
14.	Kill your television	39.	Use your magic machine
15.	Read yourself a story	40.	Get your stars out
16.	Get on your deathbed	41.	Be a finisher
17.	Be lazy to begin with	42.	Invent games
18.	Leave your friends	43.	Inner act
19.	Plan your game	44.	Live a whole life today
20.	Find your Einstein	45.	Welcome your problems
21.	Feel good first	46.	Drive a library
22.	Run toward your fear	47.	Rewind your thoughts
23.	Be unexpected	48.	Create your goals
24.	Create your relationships	49.	Get small
25.	Be where you are		

50.	Get out of the box	76.	Shine your light
51.	Advertise yourself	77.	Be a list writer
52.	Don't stop thinking	78.	Be the change
53.	Debate your dark side	79.	See the goal
54.	Make use of trouble	80.	Simplify
55.	Learn to brainstorm by yourself	81.	Pin life down
56.	Create your own voice	82.	Strengthen your purpose
57.	Live on the frontier	83.	Go on a news fast
58.	Replace your habits	84.	Choose an action
59.	Paint your day	85.	Be a thinker
60.	Swim laps under water	86.	Choose an enjoyment
61.	Coach, watch, evaluate	87.	Read mystery novels
62.	Leave home	88.	Express your thoughts
63.	Perform rituals	89.	Use your weaknesses
64.	Start life over	90.	Try becoming your problem
65.	Keep promises	91.	Inflate your goal
66.	Give some luck away	92.	Come to your rescue
67.	Draw your universe	93.	Push your own buttons
68.	Get up the game	94.	Strengthen your rehearsal
69.	Turn your mother down	95.	Improve your vision
70.	Face the sun	96.	Build your power base
71.	Look inside	97.	Link truth to beauty
72.	Go to war	98.	Take no for a question
73.	Make small change	99	Walk with love and death
74.	Do things badly	100.	Buy yourself flowers
75.	Be a visionary		

*By Steve Chandler, Printed by
Permission*

POSITIVE AFFIRMATIONS

✪ I am in control of my life and am here for a purpose.

✪ I choose to be successful.

✪ I am a great person and have great potential.

✪ I can have whatever I say and believe.

✪ I will complete every task I start.

✪ I have rock-solid confidence in my abilities.

✪ I have friends who genuinely care about me.

✪ Everything I do will prosper and I have the power to get wealth.

✪ I eject blame and negativity.

✪ I have the capacity to _____.

✪ I will be a _____ by 2014.

✪ I am productive, organized, focused, and have great time-management skills.

✪ I love myself.

✪ I will earn an honest living.

✪ I choose to take responsibility for my life.

✪ I have a great future.

✪ I am full of supernatural energy.

✪ I am an excellent listener and have great communication skills.

✪ I will be early and on time, everywhere I go.

✪ I have wisdom and choose friends who are wise.

✪ I honor my word and keep my promises.

✪ I have a good sense of humor and keep things in perspective.

✪ I am getting better and better, every day, in every way.

✪ I can follow as well as lead—I am a good team member.

✪ I am persistent, generous, loving, kind, and unique.

✪ I feel good about myself and my self-esteem is growing.

✪ I am intelligent, creative, and have common sense.

✪ I look good, I feel good, and I weigh 135 pounds.

✪ I am confident and satisfied with the level of education I have attained.

✪ I have developed a personal mission statement for my life.

✪ I have earned the respect of others and they consider my word my bond.

✪ I forgive freely rather than hold grudges.

✪ I refuse to judge other people and their values.

✪ I exercise good moral and ethical influences on others.

✪ My business standards are no different than my personal standards.

✪ I have courage to meet any challenge life may present.

✪ I am selective with the thoughts that fill my mind.

✪ I only eat healthy snacks and fruits between meals.

✪ I go to my doctor, dentist, and eye doctor at least once a year.

✪ I have power, love, and a sound mind.

✪ I drink at least six to eight glasses of water a day.

✪ I keep commitments to myself and others.

✪ I am special and feel good about myself.

✪ I was created to be prosperous, successful, and wealthy.

✪ I am selective on whom I date and whom I will marry.

✪ I will not doubt or fear what I can achieve.

✪ I believe in me and can do what I set my mind to do.

✪ My life is characterized by joy and satisfaction.

RULES FOR STUDENTS

Printed by permission.

These rules were put forth by Charles Sykes in his book Dumbing Down America. *They have floated through the Internet being attributed to Bill Gates. Most often they appear with eleven rules, leaving off three that the original author had written. Charles Sykes will be coming out with a new book expanding the rules:* 50 Rules Kids Won't Learn in School.

Rule 1: Life is not fair – Get used to it! The average teenager uses the phrase "It's not fair" 8.6 times a day. You got it from your parents, who said it so often you decided they must be the most idealistic generation ever. When they started hearing it from their own kids, they realized Rule No. 1.

Rule 2: The real world won't care as much about your self-esteem as much as your school does. It'll expect you to accomplish something before you feel good about yourself. This may come as a shock. Usually, when inflated self-esteem meets reality, kids complain that it's not fair. (See Rule No. 1.)

Rule 3: Sorry, you won't make $40,000 a year right out of high school. And you won't be a vice-president or have a car phone either. You may even have to wear a uniform that doesn't have a Gap label.

Rule 4:   If you think your teacher is tough, wait till you get a boss. He doesn't have tenure, so he tends to be a bit edgier. When you screw up, he's not going to ask you how you feel about it.

Rule 5:   Flipping burgers is not beneath your dignity. Your grandparents had a different word for burger-flipping. They called it opportunity. They weren't embarrassed to sit around talking about Kurt Cobain all weekend.

Rule 6:   It's not your parents' fault. If you screw up, you are responsible. This is the flip side of "It's my life," and "You're not the boss of me," and other eloquent proclamations of your generation. When you turn eighteen, it's on your dime. Don't whine about it, or you'll sound like a baby boomer.

Rule 7:   Before you were born, your parents weren't as boring as they are now. They got that way from paying your bills, cleaning up your room, and listening to you tell them how idealistic you are. And by the way, before you save the rainforest from the blood-sucking parasites of your parents' generation, try delousing the closet in your bedroom.

Rule 8:   Your school may have done away with the winners and losers. Life hasn't. In some schools, they'll give you as many times as you want to get the right answer. Failing grades have been abolished and class valedictorians scrapped, lest anyone's feelings be hurt. Effort is as important as results. This, of course, bears not the slightest resemblance to anything in real life. (See Rule No. 1, Rule No. 2, and Rule No. 4.)

Rule 9:   Life is not divided into semesters, and you don't get summers off! Not even Easter break. They expect you to show up every day. For eight hours. And you don't get a new life every ten weeks. It just goes on and on. While we're at it, very few jobs are interested in fostering your self-expression or helping you find yourself. Fewer still lead to self-realization. (See Rule No. 1 and Rule No. 2.)

Rule 10: Television is not real life. Your life is not a sitcom. Your problems will not all be solved in thirty minutes, minus time for commercials. In real life, people actually have to leave the coffee shop to get jobs. Your friends will not be as perky or pliable as Jennifer Aniston.

Rule 11: Be nice to nerds. You may end up working for them. We all could.

Rule 12: Smoking does not make you look cool. It makes you look moronic. Next time you're out cruising, watch an eleven-year-old with a butt in his mouth. That's what you look like to anyone over twenty. Ditto for "expressing yourself" with purple hair and/or pierced body parts.

Rule 13: You are not immortal. (See Rule No. 12.) If you are under the impression that living fast, dying young, and leaving a beautiful corpse is romantic, you obviously haven't seen one of your peers at room temperature lately.

Rule 14: Enjoy this while you can. Sure, parents are a pain, school's a bother, and life is depressing, but someday, you'll realize how wonderful it was to be a kid. Maybe you should start now. You're welcome.

"The greatest discovery of any generation is that human beings can alter their lives by altering their attitudes."
(William James)

AMERICA'S DRUG PROBLEM!

God bless mothers who drugged us!

The other day, someone at a store in our town read that a methamphetamine lab had been found in an old farmhouse in the adjoining county and he asked me a rhetorical question:

"Why didn't we have a drug problem when you and I were growing up?"

I replied: I had a drug problem when I was young:

I was drug to church on Sunday morning.

I was drug to church for weddings and funerals.

I was drug to family reunions and community socials no matter the weather.

I was drug by my ears when I was disrespectful to adults.

I was also drug to the woodshed when I disobeyed my parents, told a lie, brought home a bad report card, did not speak with respect, spoke ill of the teacher or preacher, or if I didn't put forth my best effort in everything that was asked of me.

I was drug to the kitchen sink to have my mouth washed out with soap
if I uttered a profane four-letter word.

I was drug out to pull weeds in Mom's garden and flowerbeds
and cockleburs out of Dad's fields.

I was drug to the homes of family, friends, and neighbors to help out some
poor soul who had no one to mow the yard, repair the clothesline, or chop
some firewood, and if my mother had ever known that I took a single dime
as a tip for this kindness, she would have drug me back to the woodshed.

Those drugs are still in my veins; and they affect my behavior in
everything I do, say, and think. They are stronger than cocaine, crack, or
heroin; and if today's children had this kind of drug problem, **America
would be a better place.**

Anonymous

YOU MAY BE A WORKAHOLIC:

By: Dr. Donald E. Wetmore

If you are looking forward to Christmas this year—
because you'll decide to take that afternoon off ... then you
might be a workaholic.

If twenty minutes is too long for a lunch "hour" ... you might be a
workaholic.

If hobbies are something you will get to when you "get the time" ...
you may be a workaholic.

If the color of one side of your golf bag has faded and is different
from the other side of the bag ... you might be a workaholic.

If you bring your spreadsheets to your son's football game ... you
may be a workaholic.

If you have told yourself, "I can cut back in my work hours anytime,
if I wanted to" more than three times in the last six months ... you
might be a workaholic.

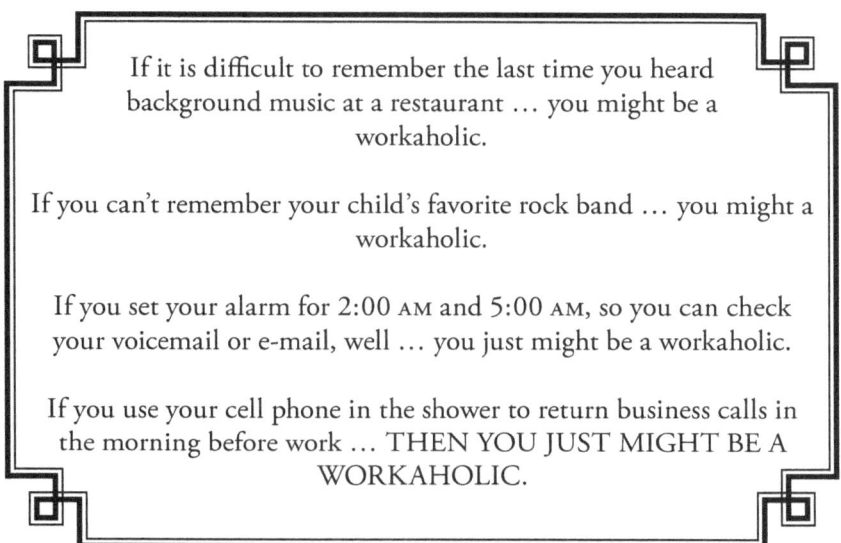

If it is difficult to remember the last time you heard background music at a restaurant ... you might be a workaholic.

If you can't remember your child's favorite rock band ... you might a workaholic.

If you set your alarm for 2:00 AM and 5:00 AM, so you can check your voicemail or e-mail, well ... you just might be a workaholic.

If you use your cell phone in the shower to return business calls in the morning before work ... THEN YOU JUST MIGHT BE A WORKAHOLIC.

DO ANY OF THESE SOUND LIKE YOU? IF SO, MAYBE WE NEED TO TAKE A TIME OUT!

(Printed by permission.)

YOU ARE SO BLESSED!!

(Something to Think About)

If you woke up this morning with more health than illness, you are more blessed than the million who won't survive the week.

If you have never experienced the danger of battle, the loneliness of imprisonment, the agony of torture, or the pangs of starvation, you are ahead of 20 million people around the world.

If you attend a church meeting without fear of harassment,
arrest, torture, or death, you are more blessed than almost
3 billion people in the world.

If you have food in your refrigerator, clothes on your back, a roof over your head, and a place to sleep, you are richer than 75 percent of this world!

If you have money in the bank and in your wallet, and spare change in a dish someplace, you are among the top 8 percent of the world's wealthy.

If your parents are still married and alive, you are very rare, especially in the United States.

If you can hold up your head with a smile on your face and are truly thankful, you are blessed—because the majority can but most do not.

If you can hold someone's hand, hug them, or even touch them on the shoulder, you are blessed because you can offer God's healing touch.

If you can read this message, you are more blessed than over 2 billion people in the world who cannot read anything at all.

You are so blessed in ways you may never know! (Anonymous)

ABOUT THE AUTHOR

For the first eight years of my life, I was raised around a small, green, spectacular country farm by my grandparents. My grandparents raised me with very strict principles and values. They often made me attend church, three times a day on Sundays. When we were bad, we were severely punished and in school. We had an outhouse in the backyard that we used for a while. We pumped water from a well, and had to heat up the water heater thirty minutes before bathing. My bedroom was the size of a small bathroom, which later became a bathroom when they remodeled the house. We lived in a house where my grandparents lived downstairs, and my aunt, uncle, and cousins lived upstairs. When we needed to make a phone call, we had to go to the post office at the bottom of the hill. Only a few people had personal phones at that time. We walked and rode our bikes everywhere we went. All the surrounding towns were about forty-five minutes apart, so there were not a lot of cars on the road. There was one of every type of business in each town. All of our needs were in walking distance. If you wanted to do real shopping, have entertainment, see castles, etc., you would drive or take the bus to the larger cities. Even though many ate fried and rich foods, due to all the walking, most of the people were in good shape.

For the good news, we had tons of fruit trees and vegetable gardens. My cousin Petra and I used to spend hours in our two favorite cherry trees. Of course, our families used all the fruits for baking and canning. Some of the special moments that I will treasure forever were the walks I took with my grandpa. For a very long time, we were the last home on top of the hill before they built more homes and streets. In the summertime, we used to walk to the very top of the hill where various flowers grew. Grandpa would always make me a crown of flowers and put it on my head, which always made me feel like a princess.

The view from the top of the hill was breathtaking. You could see the whole town and into the next. To the far right of the hill was a huge green forest. We used to get lost in there for hours, picking mushrooms and wild berries. In the winters, we used the hill for skiing and sledding. We would side step up and then ski down to the bottom, where you could then go ice-skating. Sometimes due to the snow, we were able to ski to school and use our sleds.

The week before Easter, my cousin and I would make nests in the backyard, and a few hours later, they would be filled with eggs and goodies. Since we had a farmer who lived on our street, we would go and get fresh milk every day and then play in their barn in the haystacks. Across the street from us was a huge cornfield. We would play hide-and-seek for hours. Even though we had some tough times, we had fun and great memories. The best part was all that entertainment was free.

My mom later raised me with greater responsibilities. It often seemed like I was in boot camp. Due to my strict upbringing, I became a very energetic, hard-working member of society. Therefore, I often have high expectations of other people's work ethics. As many have said, "You get out of life what you put into it." I often resented my mom for making me do so many chores all the time. However, when I ventured out on my own at the age of seventeen, I knew how to survive. A month away from turning twenty-one, I got married. I then took those values and work ethics into my marriage.

The work ethics I learned, along with time-management skills, taught me how to work two jobs at one time. My family taught me how to work for everything I wanted and needed to be successful. I will always be grateful for that. Obviously, my grandparents and parents had a vision for my life, which I later instilled in my son. We need to go back to the basics: strong work ethics, values, and family support will develop our generation of leaders tomorrow.

When writing this project, I did not intend for it to morph into a book. It began with some frustrations that I have been seeing over the years on our new generation and their work ethics or the lack thereof. When the subject of work ethics came up in one of my staff meetings, one of the employees in my office told me that I was being too hard and that maybe I should look for another job. This really offended me! I am certain he had no idea what I do, the passion I have in assisting others in employment, and the great lengths to which I will go. I make sure everyone I put to work has a résumé. If not, I write it for him or her. I want all my job seekers to be successful, regardless if the goal is finding employment or keeping it. I always assist those who are seeking employment. It does not matter if I am at home or out to dinner. Often, when I am working with students, I find out that other members of their families need jobs. I then immediately send them job leads and resources they can use.

> **"We all have a call and a purpose in this life. Those who respond to the call are always available." (Robin L. Rask)**

People who do not know you on a personal level usually have no clue what you do or who you really are. That is why there are so many who judge us. God is the ultimate judge. The irony of this is that while I was working on this project, which took three years, I was ill most of the time. There were days where I was in so much pain that I could barely walk. However, perseverance and the grace of God kept me going, along with working two full-time jobs.

> **(Matthew 19:26: "With God all things are possible.")**

I have been putting students and adults to work for more than nineteen years and have seen a drastic change in our workforce. Therefore, I began conducting a survey to see if it was just me—or were others having some similar thoughts and experiences? Lo and behold, they were and still are. Moreover, I thought maybe I could write an article to bring it to the community's awareness, and see if we cannot change this together. I also decided to use this as my professional growth project for my teaching credential. The more I began writing and receiving feedback from others, I realized this could turn into a book and we can make it a global awareness project. Since, it is not just in my town and not just in California (or, "Kaulifornia"—those of us who are from Germany speak differently).

I have worked two jobs most of my life, which takes a great deal of time-management skills, focus, and discipline. When my son David was a baby, I taught him to pick up his toys before he could walk. Therefore, he has learned good work habits ever since and is now responsible as a young adult. He will then pass these ethics on to his kids and so on and so on. That is how it should be. Hopefully, this will improve our new generation.

My dad, William O. Murphy, always used to say, "Hard work and clean living always pays off."

I may have only touched the surface on this topic, however, I hope and pray that all of you who read this can respect and appreciate this passion. It is up to us who care to make a difference and **WE ALL CAN!** There are some books available on similar topics. However, I believe that someone else may want to further research or write about this in the future.

Keep in mind: Most of this project is based on opinions and observations.

It has been said, "No one can do everything, but everyone can do something."

> **"Train a child in the way he should go, and when he is old he will not turn from it." (Proverbs 22:6, NIV)**